I Am Coldmoon: My Spiritual Odyssey

CHARLES FRODE'S "MEMOI[obscured by barcode]**d** intimacy, inspired by a Herman H[obscured] [obscured]y in Northern California. There he m[obscured]..., who became his closest male friend. Their kinship was profoundly spiritual as well as intellectual. They were fellow travelers on the winding path to transcendence: "Yet here was a man who was looking for the same elusive thing as I was—how to best live on the deepest levels of life." Frode eventually decided to leave the monastery, and thoughtfully chronicles his adventures, which include two wives, parenthood, and no shortage of erotic experimentation…the recollection's centerpiece is Frode's connection to Brother Paul; the author uses Hesse's Narcissus and Goldmund as a literary key to understanding their mutual affection…This is a strikingly candid memoir, and the author's account of Brother Paul's death—Frode was at his side when he took his last breath—is poignant…an emotionally moving homage to a beautiful friendship, a peculiarly cerebral love letter. A touching… account of a half century of brotherly love."

— Kirkus Reviews

One Times One & Other Numinous Stories of Redemption and Loss

"14 tales of madness, the possible existence of extraterrestrials, and inescapable fate. The mere title of "Imminent Doom and His Own Demise" is indicative of all the author's stories, which are decidedly darker in tone than Frode's (A Dream of India, 2015) preceding book…It likewise features a recurrent theme among the tales, one of a typically cruel destiny…As in the author's earlier work, his narratives are illustrative, even with minimal action…Often grim, but always ruminative, stories that turn out to be as eccentric as they are indelible."

– Kirkus Reviews

A Dream of India & Other Mystic Stories of Radiance and Darkness

"IN THIS DEBUT COLLECTION of short stories, characters experience spiritual awakenings through dreams and reminiscences. An epiphany, it seems, can come about by simply remembering… Memory is often a catalyst in these tales…Characters find insight in dreams as well, dream imagery that Frode generally augments with something more tangible… Metaphors are unsubtle but never clumsily so…real-world elements that usually accompany the stories' spirituality are both suitable and engrossing…Frode recurrently lingers on descriptive passages…The writing's steeped in lyricism, regardless of content… blurring the line between reality and mysticism. Inspired personal journeys that, even when traversing other worlds, stay grounded in the one readers know."

– Kirkus Reviews

I Am Goldmund:
My Spiritual Odyssey With Narcissus

I Am Goldmund:
My Spiritual Odyssey With Narcissus

Charles Frode

COPYRIGHT © 2016 BY CHARLES FRODE
All rights reserved. This book or any portion thereof may not be reproduced or used in any manner whatsoever without the express written permission of the publisher except for the use of brief quotations in a book review or scholarly journal.

First Printing: 2016
Second Printing: 2017
ISBN 978-1-365-33900-4

Excerpts from ***NARCISSUS AND GOLDMUND*** by Hermann Hesse, translated by Ursule Molinaro. Translation copyright ©1968 by Farrar, Straus & Giroux, Inc. Reprinted by permission of Farrar, Straus and Giroux, LLC.

Cover prepared by Lindsey Whitney Design, LLC
All photos and graphics by author unless otherwise end noted.

For more information about the author and his literary works visit his website at www.charlesfrodeauthorcom.

- *A Dream of India & Other Mystic Stories of Radiance and Darkness* © 2014
- *One Times One & Other Numinous Stories of Redemption and Loss* © 2015

Ordering Information:
Special discounts are available on quantity purchases by corporations, associations, educators, and others. For details contact the publisher at the address below.

Charles Frode, publisher
2389 N. Bottle Creek Place
Eagle Idaho 83616
208-340-0828
frodecharles@yahoo.com
charlesfrode@gmail.com

Dedication

This memoir is dedicated to
BROTHER PAUL WILLIAMS,
Trappist monk for 46 years until his death February 25, 2001,
My dear friend forever, my Narcissus.
I think of you always and I miss you forever.

This story is also dedicated to
MASTER HERMANN HESSE,
whose tales have held me spellbound with their truth,
and whose *Narcissus and Goldmund* has taught me more about
life and being a human being
than any other book I have ever read.

Contents

"It seemed to Goldmund that his life had been given a meaning. For a moment it was as though he were looking down on it from above, clearly seeing its three big steps: his dependence on Narcissus and his awakening; then the period of freedom and wandering; and now the return, the reflection, the beginning of maturity and harvest. It was no longer a relationship of dependence, but one of equality and reciprocity. He could be the guest of this superior mind without humiliation, since the other man had given recognition to the creative power in him." i

Hermann Hesse
Narcissus and Goldmund

Preface xi
Chapter 1: Beginning of the End 15
Chapter 2: At an Inner Altar 20
Chapter 3: Junction of Two Worlds 24
Chapter 4: First Taste 30
Chapter 5: Come Back Later 37
Chapter 6: Memos from the Monastery 44
Chapter 7: Narcissus and Goldmund 56
Chapter 8: Leaving 67
Chapter 9: Wanderer 77
Chapter 10: Soul Mate 98
Chapter 11: Helluva Honeymoon 110
Chapter 12: Curandero's Healing 129
Chapter 13: Good-bye, Narcissus 139
Chapter 14: Epilogue 144
Chapter 15: A Small Miracle 147
Chapter 16: Last Word 150
Endnotes 151

Preface

I'm both humbled and honored that you even think of the possibility of writing a book about our friendship. I must confess that I have some uneasiness about it, but at the moment I feel like waiting and seeing. Vigils, as you said, isn't a bad place to be. ii
Brother Paul Williams

  IT'S MYSTERIOUS AND HAUNTING, ISN'T IT, that at rare times in our lives we feel attracted irresistibly and against all odds to certain special people. There is a powerful species force that draws us—regardless of our circumstances—to extraordinary individuals with whom we need to harmonize and integrate ourselves. I am about to recount to you my spiritual odyssey with one of those exceptional people, a modern man, a Trappist monk. The story of our friendship is more incredible because in 1930 the Nobel Prize winning author, Hermann Hesse, wrote his world famous novel about just such a fascinating friendship between two singular and compelling medieval men—*Narcissus and Goldmund*. Let me introduce myself. I am Goldmund, and this is my story.

  Hermann Hesse's 1930 *Narcissus and Goldmund* soars as one of the 20th century's greatest psycho-spiritual novels. The story of two gifted, passionate, but dissimilar medieval men brought together in a generations-old European monastery deepens and quickens as they discover that the intellectual precision and discipline of Narcissus' ascetic mind and the inquisitiveness and generosity of Goldmund's emotional hunger have sparked an intellectual attraction and love that will grow and flourish for as long as they both live.

  It is not only the matchless and bold story of two men whose friendship and love is a model for all friendships, but it is also an articulate illumination of the themes that inspire and trouble men and women throughout the ages. *Narcissus and Goldmund* is a psychological and spiritual guide, a touchstone for seekers searching for guideposts for understanding the deepest forces underlying human nature. Friendship, sexual passion and attraction, domestic stability, the mysterious giving nature of women, men's struggle to find their emotional center, the life of the mind versus emotion, and the powerful function of art in reconciling the antagonism and contradiction of these familiar and daunting opposites that plague human beings to the end—these are authentic challenges that surface regularly in our lives as arenas for our self-realization.

It is a wonderful and profound mystery that Hesse understood the depth and width of Narcissus and Goldmund's friendship half a century before I myself embarked on the selfsame voyage of friendship and love when, at the age of twenty, I entered a Trappist monastery in northern California where I met my own Narcissus, and where I soon discovered an identical passion and understanding created from archetypical human powers brought together in one place by the unseen but powerful forces in the cosmos. This memoir is the true story of my friendship with Brother Paul and the path of spiritual friendship we have tread together for over forty-five years.

I will be utilizing excerpts from my years of correspondence with Brother Paul and direct quotations from Hesse's novel in order to illuminate and elucidate the remarkable parallels between Hesse's story and mine. Hesse wrote thoughtfully and poetically about the daily struggle to modulate and harmonize the life of the mind and the passion of art embodied in real human beings. He understood firsthand and described intimately the polar attraction of men to women with its powerful animal nature and its tender eroticism. He created moving passages describing the impermanence and precious nature of life in all its natural manifestations. Hesse's novel shimmers at every turn with the deep and vexing struggle of maintaining one's inner vitality and creativity while at the same time seeking and building physical stability and emotional security in the ephemeral world that is ours.

There are so many moving, insightful, and wondrous passages in *Narcissus and Goldmund*, and I have had to restrain my inclination to include in this memoir the numerous ones I have underlined and highlighted time and time again in my personal dog-eared copy. I consider Hesse's work to be a literary touchstone, a scripture, a road map, a textbook, for helping us come to a growing and perhaps ultimate understanding of not only our own individual personal human natures—with all our conflicts, gifts, proclivities, weaknesses, and strengths; but also the basic nature of human beings—the patterns of biological and psychological development that mold us, and the forms of struggle that determine our successes and failures.

If you have read *Narcissus and Goldmund*, you have an inkling of some of the wonderful yet disconcerting territory we will be traversing in this book. If you have not read it, buy your own copy and read it slowly, thoroughly, thoughtfully, honestly, with your heart open. Highlight the passages that call you back to reread because of their poetic splendor or because the way Hesse synthesizes ideas sparks a feeling or understanding that needs to burn and glow in you. Then pick up this sequel, my story, and be amazed at how the deep patterns of human life are repeated and manifested inexplicably for our edification and enlightenment.

I hope you enjoy learning about the many little details of daily life in a modern Trappist monastery. Hesse's book is rich in details about medieval monastic life, and much remains the same regarding the schedule and routines of work and prayer, the balance of individual and community life, and the blessings and challenges of living in the monastic environment. Yet ever since the Second Vatican Council in 1962, western monastics, particularly Trappists, have challenged themselves to be open and more communicative about their way of life, looking especially for ways to help the interested public understand why a few men and women choose to live in the so-called spiritual desert when the modern world is rushing to be connected, social, and networked. Perhaps this candid account of a powerful monastic friendship will serve to clarify further what the call to live on the deepest levels of human experience can produce in human beings.

At the end of Hesse's story, after Goldmund has returned many times from his wanderings and adventures to visit his friend at the monastery, Narcissus is finally at Goldmund's bedside as he slips away from life, one of the most moving scenes in the book.

> "Deeply shaken, Narcissus listened to his words."[iv]
>
> "'But how will you die when your time comes, Narcissus, since you have no mother? Without a mother, one cannot love. Without a mother, one cannot die'" [v]

In *my* case, I was at my dear friend, Brother Paul's bedside, *my* Narcissus, as he withdrew his life force from his body back to its origin in the cosmos. Who knows how this memoir would have unfolded if *I* had died and Brother Paul had been left behind? Perhaps it is because I am a writer that the cosmos has entrusted me with the gift of telling our story to those of you with ears to listen. We both felt that it is a story well worth telling. I wish Master Hesse was alive so that I might bow to him in recognition of the truth of his and of our story.

In both this memoir and Hesse's *Narcissus and Goldmund* you have an opportunity to dig deep, deeper, and discover something priceless about yourself. There is no need to live in a monastery to experience the deepest levels of yourself, of humanity. As you will come to understand in this memoir, your monastery is in your heart. In the very same way that physicists describe how every point in the universe is expanding as if every point was the center, so too wherever you are, you are at the center of the action, the cosmic action, *your* action, ready, primed. There is no need at all to go somewhere else to find something you feel is elusive, out there. There is only the need to respond to the call within yourself to go deeper within. There it is.

You have everything you need to start. The inner light you find within yourself will be as startling and illuminating as you let it be.

Chapter 1: Beginning of the End

"'My dear friend,' he whispered, 'I cannot wait until tomorrow. I must say farewell to you now, and as we part I must tell you everything.'" vi
"If I know nevertheless what love is, it is because of you. I have been able to love you, you alone among all men. You cannot imagine what that means. It means a well in a desert, a blossoming tree in the wilderness. It is thanks to you alone that my heart has not dried up, that a place within me has remained open to grace.'" vii
Herman Hesse
Narcissus and Goldmund

All I ask of you is forever to remember me as loving you. viii
Brother Paul Williams

    Two astonishing and transcendent whirlwinds —one public and one private—punctuated the end of my earthly relationship with Brother Paul. But before those twin mystical events could augur the writing of this memoir—on a too perfect, blue-skied mid-Sunday morning in February of 2001, in the middle of flipping a flawless crepe onto the warming plate in the oven, my cell phone began buzzing irritatedly against the counter, and I struggled to get the thin pancake doubled over onto the hot plate in one piece and still get the call because I sensed an odd urgency in the moment. That call would signal the beginning of the end.

    "Can I speak to Charles Frode please? This is Brother John at New Clairvaux monastery."

    Why is Brother John calling me after so many years of being away from the...Oh, my God! Something's wrong with Paul...

    I had fled the monastery years ago, and I'd been blissfully married to a modern Aztec princess, my dear wife, Elvira, for thirteen years. I'd driven up to see my old friend, Brother Paul, several months previous during the summer break from teaching creative writing to budding 10th grade public school authors, and I spent a few days at the monastery visiting with him in our characteristic way. In the chilly early hours before 6 am Mass and then work, we would huddle in his tiny office in the old brick barn and talk of old times and new life. If he was able to take off work that day, we would spend all morning walking the familiar north-south, east-west gravel roads through the prune or walnut fields, or—if it was too hot—using one of the cool guest houses for our dialogue and reminiscence.

While walking out by Deer Creek on the north side of the monastery where Ishi's people hunted, fished, and left there fragments of their lives, Paul mentioned that he had a persistent pain in his side that had been bothering him, but he played it down in his characteristically modest way and instead complained of old age aches and pains. We continued to talk of the many authentic ways of experiencing God, what it means to love all kinds of other people, the blessings of my marriage with my dear Elvira, my children and their personalities and proclivities, the future of the monastic life both Eastern and Western, and how each of us was growing in our individual lives of prayer, silence, spiritual presence. I left Brother Paul with a long embrace, affirmations of our friendship and the love for each other we had always kept protected and private, and along with sincere promises to write, but not email, heavens, not email!

"Charles, I'm sorry to be calling you like this but. . ."

Brother John had known Paul since the early fifties when they and a score of brother monks had ventured out from Kentucky's 150 year-old Gethsemani Abbey to found a daughter monastery in California, and I knew the two had been friends.

I sensed what he was going to say before he added, "I know Paul told you he was ill...but I thought you should know that he has slipped into a coma and is unconscious and I...I thought you might want to come up here while you still have a chance to..."

I called the substitute teacher service right after the last crepe, arranged for someone, anyone, to take my classes for three days, and the next morning I was humping the speed limit on Highway 101 and then Interstate 5 north up the midsection of California to tiny, out-of-the-way Vina between Sacramento and Corning. As I left the outskirts of Salinas in the middle of what would turn out to be my family's last year in California, I recalled the many other times I had bussed and then later driven up eagerly and excitedly to the monastery to visit my friend. This time I knew there would be no walking, no talking, no embracing, no reminiscing, no sharing of lives because Paul had pancreatic cancer, and it was the end. Brother John was one of the few at the monastery who knew of my friendship and love for Brother Paul, and I felt his usual graciousness and love in calling me to inform me that they had sedated my Narcissus for the pain, and that he was unconscious to the world.

Who would I find, what would I say to my Narcissus, what did I expect to do if he was unconscious, what would happen when I arrived at the monastery?

No one noticed when I steered slowly through the quiet little town of Vina onto the back street that led to the monastery. I didn't see a soul as I drove through the stone gate and parked by the guest houses. Nobody bicycled down to greet me and get me situated in a  guesthouse room. Not one person would remember me except for a few monks who were still alive there— the novice master, the abbot, a few others perhaps, Brother John, of course. I wandered to the shade of one of the huge old maples and sat in one of the simple benches located for the view out across the new vineyards.

My mind wandered here and there around the monastery grounds where I, we, had strolled together, worked together, learned about ourselves, embraced and cried together, prayed and meditated, but my consciousness paid no attention to the memories. I was in a no-man's-land of waiting, emptiness, attending to the ultimate focus of friendship and love, the never and the always of these ultimate events, just sitting on the hard, weathered bench, waiting for someone, waiting for no one, waiting alone, waiting with everyone in the world who ever waited.

"Hello...has anyone helped you?" I didn't know the voice, nor did I recognize the monk who was walking over to mercifully pop the fragile bubble of my mental exile.

"Of course, I will let Brother John know that you are here; he's expecting you. You knew Brother Paul when you were here before?"

Time in a monastery is unhurried except at harvest time, and even then time is treated not as an enemy but more as a teacher. Brother John pedaled down under the huge maples an hour later, parked his rickety balloon-tired cruiser, and called out my name as he strode over to where I was still sitting flooded in reverie where the flotsam of melancholy would bump painfully into my heart now and then, and the jetsam of vivid images of my time at the monastery accumulated until I realized that some part of me still belonged there, even if for just a few more days, a few more hours. The always innocently smiling monk and I embraced, exchanged small talk a brief moment, then he shocked me.

"We just got word from the doctor that no one can see Paul. He's unconscious in the infirmary, and no one knows how much longer he has. So they're limiting..."

I thought of the days, weeks, months, years I had not taken the time to visit my dear friend Brother Paul, the one with whom I was eternally tied in silence now as a spiritual partner—mind and heart, passion and prayer, intellectual man and feeling man, my Narcissus and his Goldmund. I thought of the letters I had waited too long to answer, thought of loving so many other people, loving that relegated little-by-little the love we had for each other to an overlooked corner of my heart. I thought of never seeing Paul again, and I was devastated.

"Isn't there some way I can...?" There have been a few times in my life when I have begged, implored, entreated someone for something I needed desperately.

"I will see what I can do, Charles...In the meantime, let me show you your room, and if there is any hope, I will come and get you."

I sat in the cool, sparse, air conditioned concrete block room and thumbed through my worn, underscored, and dog-eared copy of *Narcissus and Goldmund* pausing here and there at the heavy underlining, reading whatever caught my eye, musing over the events of life, realizing that Paul and I had lived out fully and deeply the archetype that Hermann Hesse so sensitively fleshed out in his book. I had never anywhere else read of such a forceful friendship, and Paul and I had been careful not to share the personal and archetypical power of our friendship with just anyone. Only Brother John and the abbot knew of our friendship, and I was counting on that to open the infirmary door to Paul's room.

I awoke later from deep sleep to a quiet but firm knocking on the door of the small guest room. It was dusk, and Brother John was insistent that I hurry down to see Paul before the evening meal. As I walked through the cloister, I looked for the familiar, the comforting—the covered cloister walkway, the family orchard, the door into the cool church. I noticed the new—several faces I didn't recognize, the infirmary, and I felt like both an intimate and a stranger at the same time as Brother John ushered me into the new infirmary building so cool and quiet. He opened the nearest door for me, touched my shoulder and nodded that I should enter, then quietly closed the door after me.

Chapter 2: At an Inner Altar

"Natures of your kind, with strong, delicate senses, the soul-oriented, the dreamers, poets, lovers are almost always superior to us creatures of the mind. You take your being from your mothers. You live fully; you were endowed with the strength of love, the ability to feel. Whereas we creatures of reason, we don't live fully; we live in an arid land, even though we often seem to guide and rule you. Yours is the plenitude of life, the sap of the fruit, the garden of passion, the beautiful landscape of art. Your home is the earth; ours is the world of ideas. You are in danger of drowning in the world of the senses; ours is the danger of suffocating in an airless void. You are an artist; I am a thinker. You sleep at the mother's breast; I wake in the desert. For me the sun shines; for you the moon and the stars. Your dreams are of girls; mine of boys." ix
Hermann Hesse
Narcissus and Goldmund

You are grateful for this gift and will nurture it well. A gift coming from God yet welling up from the depths of who you are, since God ordinarily works that way: quietly in the humdrum, out of our own depths which we co-create with Him as we play with Him in the loveliness of His creation. x
Brother Paul Williams

  THIS YOUNG CHARLES WAS A BOY for whom silence was a natural state. Comfortable silence, accommodating, where thoughts could find their own way to the surface of his nascent awareness and then onto deeper months and years of understandings. Where the silence made space for him to draft mental and then paper plans for what he would do about that understanding— three-dimensional schema, material lists, then task analyses and timetables for action. Model cars and boats made from scratch, drawings and graphics, reflective poems, books books and more books, inventions, puttering, cooking, skating, skateboarding, bicycle riding, all alone, never lonely, filled with silence.

Sounds entered Charles' sanctuary of silence with not only vivid, visual, and familiar three-dimensional coordinates for their contexts, but also comforting emotional associations that intersected unconsciously within his soul and made non-verbal connections that seemed to be second nature to the boy, and that became in reality newly constellated impressions, interpretation, and insights. Airplanes overhead Saturday at high noon, lawn mowers interrupting the dusk calm, friends shouting at play outside, crickets and frogs in the moist evening twilight, silence empty of sound, silence full of silence, all provided the foundation and design for his inner world.

Charles soon found that his ten-speed bicycle offered him a way to move more deeply into silence, into mindlessness, into focus without conceptualization, straight ahead, head down, cranking one breath after another. He discovered that in pushing and pulling the simple machine, in the whirl of wheels and gears, in the familiar clicks, hums, squeaks, tuned cables, and lever detents, and in the surfaceless and thoughtless effort, in all the intimacies and intricacies of his team issue celeste Bianchi, he wound his personal meditation into fatigue and emptiness. He would leave the morning mists of Stockton and wheel through Linden, Belota, Valley Springs, San Andreas, Mokelumne Hill, Jackson, and on past Fiddletown, or into Angels Camp, and Murphys, and then past Lake Alpine. Later he would venture on to higher and more challenging Tioga Pass, Spooner Summit, Carson Pass, Lake Tahoe, Echo Summit, Luther, and Carson Passes. He slept under the stars, off the road, after forty or eighty miles a day, on his way, however far.

Charles later followed his family to Santa Cruz where the cycles of the ocean became his meditation. In the lows and highs of the daily tides, the variations and uniformity of swells, the offshore and onshore breezes, the exposure and creatures of intertidal zones, the forces that create waves and beaches — in these essential fluctuations of the maternal source he discovered an unspoken analog to his mind. In the challenge of the waves he found lessons about living — about waiting and then seizing opportunities, about favorable and unfavorable conditions, about danger and the value of fear, about the environments out of which action takes shape, about when to keep a distance and when to approach, about cooperating and resisting. He also learned the spontaneity of movement without thought, how resistance influences movement, the nature and utilization of a surface's friction, the hydrodynamics of his body soaring through tons of pumping angled green water. He spent hours and years in the water, joyful times of surfing, observing, absorbing and doing — the water, his willing teacher. There would be many teachers in his life, as he himself would become.

    Throughout this youthful time of doing, absorbing, and learning Charles had also been observing the rituals, acquiring and reinforcing within himself the symbols, and probing within his mind and body the fecund secrets of the Roman Catholic religion. Acolyte at the neighborhood church from the early age of seven, he packed daily and weekly doses of liturgical gratitude and healing into himself until the age of twenty. The parish priest was a family friend, and he would pick up Charles at 5:30 am to assist at his personal daily Mass. The devout teenager would be selected frequently for significant church ceremonies such as Lenten and Easter liturgies, marriages, and funerals. He would ride his bicycle to daily Mass rain or shine where he read the various scriptural passages for the congregation. It was understandable, although ultimately fruitless, that the diocesan priests would be rubbing their hands together in anticipation of Charles becoming one of them.

    For Charles there were always the waxed and fragrant hardwood surfaces; big, heavy, cool brass candle holders; large smooth pearl-white candles; elaborate gold chalices and sacred vessels; bittersweet incense pouring aromatic smoke from the end of the swaying chained censer; sleek intricately embroidered and appliquéd vestments each with symbolic significance and each corresponding to its day in the liturgical calendar; predictable and stylized bows, genuflections, and gestures; antiphonal exchanges between priest and altar boy with vicarious intent; the many contrived limits of location and purpose that delineated and marked the sacred from the temporal. Daily and monthly rhythms of the church's liturgical drama flooded Charles, and the young man swam comfortably with the currents of icon, symbol, and ceremony — never against the flow but always allowing the antiphonal systole and diastole of words and actions to create meaning deep within him.

It was as if this was another ocean of waves and beaches to him, another bicycle trip up and over the next high mountain pass. On the Bianchi, swimming out through the surf line, or at the altar, it was no different really. Charles had learned to let the moment's focus of practiced attention clear and open his mind to the other business at hand. He had no complex cognates, no multisyllabic terms, and no esoteric explanations for all this. The words would come later, much later, now perhaps as he writes these words, and in spite of the fact that they would be a wonder to him, he would let go of words eventually to find what was deeper. This, though, was the first order of business, the business of building and clearing away, the training of focusing and defocusing, the balance of doing and non-doing, the true work.

It was to this business that the monastery beckoned the boy. The call was quiet but insistent. It summoned him north, and it said, "Alone."

Chapter 3: Junction of Two Worlds

"They rode through the chill of late autumn, and one day, on a morning when the bare trees hung thick with frost, they rode across a wide rolling land of deserted reddish moors, and the long chains of hills looked strangely familiar, and then came a high elm wood and a little stream and an old barn at the sight of which Goldmund's heart began to ache in happy anguish." xi

"But now they were approaching their goal, and after a few days they had reached it. Shortly before tower and roofs of the cloister became visible, they rode across the fallow stony fields." xii

Hermann Hesse
Narcissus and Goldmund

Yes, Deer Creek still runs down by the cannery, the roads still skirt the different fields, the little red and orange plums still grow on the trees far from the monastery buildings, the winters are still bone-chilling and the summers hot as hell. My office is still in the big brick barn, "the winery," though in a different room since I have a different job. But the prune trays are not stacked by the ovens. The ovens are gone, as are most of the trays. We ran the dipper and dehydrator for the last time in 1979. Now we haul the prunes directly from the orchards to the Sunsweet dryer in Corning. When I walk through the old dipper area now, stripped of its machinery, a painful nostalgia grips my guts and won't let go. xiii

Brother Paul Williams

TWENTY ARID MILES BELOW BAKERSfiELD, California, State Highway 99 ventures off boldly on its own, due north, leaving its younger bully twin, Interstate 5, to skirt the eastern side of the coastal mountain range along the western edge of California's wide and fertile San Joaquin Valley. Interstate Highway 5 skims along barely touching the gentle foothills and looks down across acres of perfectly straight rows of orange, walnut, almond, and apricot orchards. Through Buttonwillow, Kettleman City, and Gustine two black and virile northbound lanes of macadam undulate, diverge, and merge again with their southerly counterparts.

 Steering through mile after numbing mile of seventy-mile-an-hour, cruise-controlled trance states, drivers daydream, meditate, and anticipate the next rest or fast food stop impatient to relieve the boredom and fatigue of driving full-out and straight-on for three hours. Passengers catch sight of the wide and cool looking California Aqueduct and its many intersecting irrigation canals that carry precious liquid gold that falls generously on the northern half of the state down to the arid and grateful southern half of the state. Along the way farmers siphon off their expensive and continuously diminishing allocation of water to irrigate fields of chiles, peppers, tomatoes, alfalfa, beets, and carrots. Along Highway 5 only the blind do not see how essential the politics of water distribution has been in converting bleak grassland into an oasis of fertility and productivity, and how devastating a few years of drought have been on the state that used to be called optimistically the Golden State.

 Interstate 5 shuttles the state's busy urban dwellers quickly and efficiently all the way from the dense southern megalopolises of San Diego and Los Angeles through the long valley corridor up to the northern urban giants, the deteriorating inland port of Stockton and the golden state capital of Sacramento. All roads, local, state, and interstate, seem to merge or disappear in either Stockton or Sacramento because most east-west traffic between the jewels of Lake Tahoe and San Francisco speeds through this narrow and heavily populated midsection of California. The Interstate veers west out of Sacramento into the northern half of what is now Sacramento Valley.

 Through tiny agricultural enclaves such as Yolo, Dunnigan, Arbuckle, Williams, Maxwell, Willows, and Orland, the grey, multi-lane artery snubs Vina and the monastery and finally arrives in lush

Redding where anyone could be tempted beyond their ability to resist detouring into the lush green mountains on either side. A trip west along scenic 299 to Whiskey Town, French Gulch, Junction City, and Burnt Ranch or east to Enterprise, Bella Vista, Ingot, Hatchet Mountain Summit, or Fall River Mills could delay a driver weeks, fly fishermen even longer. Interstate 5 avoids the temptation and climbs up and out of the Golden State through Dunsmir, past the fourteen-thousand foot crystal mystery of Mount Shasta, through Weed and Yreka, and out northernmost Horn Peak at Hilt into Oregon.

Where Interstate 5 leaves Highway 99 back down below Bakersfield, the older 99, on the other hand, continues patiently north to stop and start again in scores of cotton and tomato towns where sunburned men, women, and children wrestle the sun, dust, wind, government regulations, and large agribusiness monopolies for the harvest. Corner markets, machine shops, tractor supplies, small libraries, numbered grange halls, tiny elementary schools, and vestigial five and dime stores document the tenacity and endurance of two and three generations of farmers, big men and strong women still, on family farms now shrinking and disappearing, a way of life barely profitable anymore.

Drive through Delano, where Cesar Chavez epitomized the dignity and struggle of farmworkers through his revitalization of non-violence; Visalia and Fresno, dual gateways to Kings Canyon National Park; Chowchilla, where State Highway 152 cuts left across the plain to Los Banos, and where that wide, heavily traveled highway climbs up to Pacheco Pass past Dinosaur Point by San Luis Reservoir and on the way to Gilroy (the odoriferous Garlic Capital of the world), Mission San Juan Bautista (and its panoramic view of the San Andreas Fault), tiny Castroville (self-proclaimed Artichoke Capital of the world), John Steinbeck's burgeoning Salinas Valley (where lettuce and broccoli are king), and the world famous marine sanctuary and tourist mecca of Monterey Bay (skirted by Steinbeck's Cannery Row); and through the gateway town of Merced, where scenic 140 winds historically into the John Muir's valley of spectacular and overcrowded Yosemite National Park.

Thirty minutes to the north in Stockton and an hour later in Sacramento Highway 99 parallels Interstate 5 through more densely populated, agro-industrial towns. But ten miles out of Sacramento at Rio Linda the four and sometimes eight lanes of 5 veer sharply to the west, and 99 angles its two to four rows of traffic to the east as if the two highways were trying to sidestep to avoid each other. As they bulge out from one another, they flank the Sacramento River on each side until they can no longer dodge each other at Red Bluff where 99 gives up without fanfare, losing its dominance without a fight to the younger, buffed out and aggressive 5.

Fifteen country miles before 99 yields to 5, even before the numbers 99 and 5 meant highway or freeway, down below the high 1000 Lakes Valley Wilderness, 10,457 foot Mount Lassen, and the water-sanctified Plumas National Forest, the last survivor of the Yahi Indians stumbled along Mill Creek into the curious 1916 world of the white European settlers. Like his people there for hundreds and perhaps thousands of years before him, Ishi [xiv] lived, and then abruptly succumbed to exposure to the white man who in fifty years had infected, enslaved, and shot 20,000 of his people. Ishi's people disappeared one by one with no one to notice until only he remained, and then he too vanished.

Unnoticed in the same area now, a quarter mile off the side of two lane Highway 99 that cuts through that history-rich area, the out-of-the-way town of Vina withers slowly like the plums left unnoticed or ignored in the neighboring orchards, desiccated, and almost forgotten. During the 1850's miners and Chinese railroad workers stumbled down to the civilization of the valley from the gold camps and digs in the Sierra Nevada Mountains, from places they called Rich Bar, Goodyears Bar, Shingletown, Hat Creek, Rough and Ready, and Graniteville. They would come with leather pouches full of gold dust and gold nuggets they had washed out of the river and creek beds, gold they gambled for whisky with the shrewd Chinese barkeeps or for female companionship with Vina's elegant eastern-born madam.

The miners and workers kept Vina prosperous until gold petered out before the century turned. Hundreds of Chinese railroad workers and miners stayed around Vina to work in the nearly four-thousand acre vineyards that Leland Stanford had established in the 1880's. Governor of California, millionaire rail tycoon, and founder of his namesake university, Stanford was among the many easterners who arrived in the wide valley to settle, subdue, and develop the area, and to cut down the valley's millions of indigenous oaks for fuel and timber; in their place he planted orchard after orchard of grapes, walnuts, almonds, plums, peaches, and olives. Their grandchildren now level, irrigate, and harvest that same productive ground.

"You wanna get off here?" the Greyhound driver yelled back over his shoulder.

"Is that Vina over there?" the novice bus rider called up to the driver as he spied a water tower looming ahead. He got up from his seat and stood by the driver who was downshifting in anticipation of having to drop off his passenger.

"Yep, that's Vina...'bout a mile off the road," the driver replied to the question and pointed, "and that's Vina Junction up ahead. I can drop you off here by the side of the road, but you gotta walk into town."

"Yes, please. I have to get off there, thanks," the boy said, grateful to have arrived after six uncomfortable hours on what he had naively thought was the express bus. From his hometown in Stockton the middle-aged grey bus had taken him into and through every possible city, town, and unnamed bus stop possible between his home and Vina. He had stretched his legs and bought snacks in several sleepy bus stops along the route and looked at every possible new thing he could catch sight of out the smudged windows.

The bus ground into low gear and slowed to a crawl, crossed the broken line that divides Highway 99's northbound and southbound lanes, lugged to a bumpy stop, and idled off the shoulder of the road.

"You goin' t' the monastery?" the driver asked. As the young man pulled his backpack down from the luggage rack and nodded his head, the driver surprised him with, "Like to visit there myself someday, yuh know?...Everyone just goes down there," the driver pointed in the direction of the unassuming one lane road that intersected the highway. "Well... good luck," he added as he waited for the boy to step down off the bus.

The diesel motor spewed foul smelling smoke as it lurched and tottered back out onto the road north leaving Charles standing alone on the gravel edge of nowhere. *Well,* he reassured himself, *I made it...I'm finally here.* He looked around, and then started walking slowly away from the highway towards what he hoped would be his future.

A few families, a general store, and a post office still cling to the sides of the short, shaded main street of Vina. Life is quiet and unperturbed as time in Vina slows and isolates itself from distant  farming neighbors and fields. A long thin road, 7th Street, borders the sleepy little town on the north and crosses up and over the railroad track that constrains the chaos and commotion of the freight trains that pass several times a day behind Vina. It was down this road that 18 year old Charles followed what his mother always said was the Treat Family aquiline nose for twenty minutes walking slowly by the plain white cross on the left, then around the eucalyptus-lined bend in the road, and finally down the last three-hundred yards to the silent grey stone arch of the monastery gate.

Chapter 4: First Taste

"Outside the entrance of the Mariabronn cloister, whose rounded arch rested on slim double columns, a chestnut tree stood close to the road." xv

"The beautiful treetop—secret kin to the portal's slender sandstone columns and the stone ornaments of the window vaults and pillars, loved by the Savoyards and Latins—swayed above the cloister entrance." xvi

Hermann Hesse
Narcissus and Goldmund

NO ONE MET HIM AT THE MONASTERY GATE. In fact, Charles couldn't see anyone, no monks, nobody waiting for him over by those little rundown clapboard ranch houses or anywhere else that he could make out.

What am I supposed to do, he wondered, *just walk in? Where is everyone?*

The Greyhound had left Charles by the side of the road at 5:30. By the time he reached the gate, it was six, a chilly evening, and the April overcast continued stubbornly to refuse the sun an appearance. He put his bag down, reached out his hand and felt the cold chiseled granite of the arched gate. The stone was the same shade of grey as the sky, except this rock sky had flecks of black, like tiny pitch-black stars set densely over the entire irregular surface of the gate. Whoever made the gate had finished the mortar between each course and block with perfectly tooled half-inch concave joints. Charles ran his hand along one of the mortar joints and let his finger listen for irregularities in the depth of the mortar, but the joint was silent and smooth.

Perfect. I guess the monks built this, he mused as he waited.

He broke off his train of thought as he snooped around the gate looking for a date, a name, some kind of marker or identification. He found none, except, of course, the evenly proportioned words chiseled into the face of the arch: Our Lady of New Clairvaux Abbey. At the side of the arch he noticed a piece of steel conduit protruding about four feet from the grass. At the end was an electrical junction box, and in the center of its faceplate Charles spied a small, round, white button that appeared to be a doorbell or buzzer. He pushed the button and heard a bell clanging somewhere in one of the farmhouses farther inside the gate. It sounded like an old-fashioned telephone, loud and grating, disturbing the quiet setting where he was beginning to feel like an uninvited intruder.

No one came out of the farmhouse, and no one came to the gate. Charles waited several minutes before he rang the offensive bell again. He felt like an idiot to be interrupting the peace and calm of the monastery, and he began to entertain the idea of turning around and walking back to wherever he had had the temerity to come from, when he noticed someone coming towards him. Far down the end of the road inside the cloister a monk appeared to be weaving a bicycle slowly back and forth towards the gate.

Finally...Charles thought. He felt relieved as he peered at the approaching monk. He watched the man transform gradually from an amorphous black and white blob to a smiling, bespectacled young man rather oddly riding a big old balloon-tire bicycle.

"I'm Brother Michael, the guest master," the monk said as he glided to a stop and extended his hand.

Charles shook it firmly and introduced himself. "I hope you didn't have to wait too long," the brother explained as he got off his blue and white cruiser and picked up Charles' bag from the ground.

"We were all in the refectory eating, and I didn't hear the bell. I walked outside and spied you standing here. I hope you didn't have to wait too long. We just don't have too many guests arriving in the evening...and we expected you earlier...But, please, come in, we have a room in the guest house ready for you."

The two young men strolled side by side through the gate and into the guest area. Charles realized that Brother Michael could have been a couple of years older than he was, but not that much older.

I wonder how old you have to be, Charles wondered, *to be a monk in this place.*

The two young men made small talk about each other's life, Brother Michael handed Charles a typewritten schedule of the monastic day, and then he invited his guest into the guest house kitchen to make him an impromptu meal.

Before the nineteenth century turned twenty, and before the monks bought the property for their monastery, Leland Stanford  had built four small but ample clapboard bunk houses on his ranch. Each little whitewashed building had a porch, a small front living room with wood stove, and a hallway that divided the house into two sections. Each half of the bunk house had four rooms and a bathroom. One of the bunk houses was larger because it housed the main ranch kitchen, dining area, and offices. It was in this building that Charles sat alone at a long wooden table and waited for Brother Michael to bring him whatever he was preparing up in the kitchen.

"Can I help you, Brother?" Charles finally called into the kitchen.

"Sure, can you cut bread?" Brother Michael called back.

The young brother set his guest to sawing off thick whole wheat slices from the largest, most voluptuous loaf of bread Charles had ever seen. The brother told him that old arthritic Father Vincent baked ten or fifteen of the loaves every day to feed the hungry monks.

"You have your own bakery?" Charles inquired.

"Oh, we're pretty well self-sufficient here," the monk-cook replied as he beat several eggs to a froth.

"We have a bakery that's always busy...uh... Brother Adam's shoe shop stays warm over the laundry so his arthritis doesn't bother him so much, and the cannery over by Deer Creek...That's where we put away apples, pears, plums, and apple butter...Can you hand me that spatula, please?"

Brother Michael was assembling a cheese omelet for Charles, and the two young men focused their attention on the smells of the toasting bread and melting cheddar. When they finally set their work on the dining room table, Charles listened as the brother blessed his and the food's safe arrival. Brother Michael commenced his overview of the monastery as Charles tried to maintain what he imagined was monastic decorum while he devoured the simple but sumptuous meal.

"Yes," Brother Michael continued in his characteristically methodical pronunciation of each syllable, "the monks arrived here in Vina in 1955. They were sent here from Kentucky to build a new monastery with the surplus monks from Gethsemani Abbey. There used to be a big vineyard here before we arrived...In fact, these guest houses down here and our brick barn are from those days. Yes, lots of history here… More eggs, Charles?"

"I can't, Brother," Charles apologized, "I've already eaten too much, but it's so good. Thank you for cooking for me."

"You like turkey eggs, eh?" Brother Michael laughed at Charles' consternation, then added, "You want to help me clean up?

In twenty minutes the two young men had returned the kitchen to its previous wooden, porcelain, and stainless steel state. In another ten minutes Brother Michael had walked Charles to the second bunk house where he learned that he was the only occupant until the weekend when a dozen or so visitors were expected to take up temporary residence. Brother Michael began to excuse himself, said that Vespers and then Compline would be starting at 7:30, pointed out the path that Charles could take to the monastic church if he wanted to attend the last community ceremony of the day, and then bid his guest good-night.

Charles sat down on the bed to gather his thoughts. The mattress slumped down farther than he imagined any box springs could sag before it hit the floor, and he knew that sleep was not going to be one of the luxuries he would enjoy during his stay in the guest house. It would be three years before Charles would climb the narrow, steep stairs of the cloister and find his way to his cubicle in the monks' dormitory where the thin cotton batting mattress never sagged because it rested on thick, unyielding wooden boards. It would be no luxury either, but it would be a tiny and welcome sanctuary to the young man after a day of prayer and work with twenty-five other monks.

Up at 3:15, then Matins at 2:30, the early morning chanting of psalms in the dark church; then individual prayer, study, and buffet breakfast until 6 o'clock communal Mass; individual prayer and study until 9 when work started and continued until 12:15; community prayer, then supper, and a siesta if one wanted until 1:00; return to work till 3 or 4; a simple buffet dinner and individual prayer and study; and finally the poignant chanting and singing of Vespers and Compline to complete the day at 8 sharp. Although he had barely enough room to stretch out his arms in the small sleeping cubicle, it was the only place he would be by himself.

Charles was alone now though. He looked at his watch and decided it was too late to attend the last community ceremony of the day. He put his bag on the desk and opened it. After he hung his coat on the back of the chair, he looked around, and took visual inventory of the little room. Old fashioned desk lamp, alarm clock, one towel, wooden chair and desk, crucifix, and 1963 calendar on the wall, extra blanket. He was tired from the duration and uncertainty of the bus trip. He took off his shoes and lay back on the soft yielding bed.

Yearning aroused imagination within Charles' mind, and he wondered if the monks' life at New Clairvaux Abbey was like it was pictured in all the books he had been reading and rereading. Charles had initially nurtured and sustained himself with all of Thomas Merton's wildly popular books about the monastic life. His best-selling books about Trappist monasteries, monastic life, prayer, contemplation, and the idealized photographs in the books fired Charles' eagerness to lead a life of work, study, and prayer. Merton became the epitome of monastic life and spiritual development for two generations. The post-World War Two generation sought balance to the horrors of World War Two within the walls of monasteries where silence and peace healed the vestiges of violence and destruction that remained within them. Then the baby boomers found Merton to be the exemplar of modern man — well-educated and well-read, affirming of the Christian heritage and religion, open and eager to accommodate Eastern spiritualties and ways of thinking, engaged in constructive social protest and change, challenging monastics to find renewed relevance in the contemporary world, and encouraging and modeling how one could live a contemplative life in and out of the monastery.

Before Charles finished imagining that some of the monks at the monastery might have met or known Thomas Merton, the young guest drifted into silent sleep, sleep far from the noise and lights of the city, rural sleep, farm sleep, the welcome sleep of arrival and accomplishment. He awakened twice during the night. A freight train disturbed the monastic silence when it chugged, hissed, and clickety-clacked past the monastery at 11:30. Charles thought it was going to plow through the guest house, it was that loud and close. The second event woke him—a dream. He sat straight up, looked at the eerie, numinous green numbers on the face of the alarm clock, and tried to replay the dream with as much detail as he could remember at 5:56 a.m.

A castle...really a stone fortress on a hill. Under the fortress, in a deep basement or secret chamber, scores of small, powerful, mole-like soldiers carrying spears marched furtively and covertly in columns up to the top of the fortress battlements where they formally presented the waiting dreamer with special weapons like spears or swords which he would be needing to do spiritual battle.

Many years later Charles would remember this dream as the first of many messages that he would be receiving from his deepest self, dreams such as this one about preparation and investiture for spiritual struggle, or a later one where he was riding a white stallion through huge, smooth waves in the open sea to discover and rescue his mother from the bottom of the ocean. Years after he had finally entered and then ultimately left New Clairvaux Abbey, he would continue to be graced with dreams about the monastery; dreams about the deep roots the monastery and monks had grown down into his awareness and world view; dreams about his kinship and intimacy with the places and feelings he had fleshed out during his time there; and most importantly, dreams that reassured him that although, like Goldmund, he would ultimately choose not to return to the monastic buildings, schedules, routines, and family, he would never really leave the monastic spirit. He would have discovered and continued to carry and nurture the monastery in his heart. Saintly Father Timothy would make sure of that on Charles' last day of monastery.

Charles wrote down the dream as well as he could remember, put on his shoes, went to the bathroom to splash icy water on his face, and walked down the bunk house steps into his first day of monastery.

Chapter 5: Come Back Later

I look forward to having you visit us whenever is convenient. Let me know the dates as far in advance as possible, since we need to reserve a room for you in the guest area, and they stay pretty well booked up down there most of the time. Rooms are more available during the week than on weekends, so you can arrange to come on Monday afternoon or Tuesday, and stay till Thursday afternoon or Friday morning, that would be our best bet. [xvii]
Brother Paul Williams

ABBEY OF NEW CLAIRVAUX · VINA · CALIFORNIA · 96092

22 November 1966

Dear Charley,

You are most welcome to come for a visit any time you can find it convenient to do so; we have plenty of room in our guesthouse.

Just let me know in advance when to expect you, so that I can notify the guestmaster.

You will be able to see the life of the monastery, and I can discuss your vocation with you - even though you have not reached the age limit of 20 which is necessary before entering.

We will keep your vocation in our prayers.

In Christ our Brother,

Fr. Joseph Wittbrod, O.C.S.O.

IT HAD TAKEN A WHILE for seventeen-year old Charles to straighten things out. Not so much with himself, but with everyone around him. The parish priests wanted him, and the Franciscans who ran Charles' high school recognized a vocation when they saw one. They were all informative, persuasive, and well-intentioned, but once Charles discovered the Trappist monastic life, he knew what he wanted. He had unearthed a list of Trappist monasteries and discovered that New Clairvaux Abbey was only a few hundred miles to the north of his home town. Not only was he sure about the Trappists, but he also began planning to visit New Clairvaux as soon as spring vacation rolled around.

The guest master had replied to Charles' first inquiry with a short typewritten note inviting and welcoming Charles to visit any time, see the life of the monastery, and discuss his vocation with the novice master. The priest closed with "We will keep your vocation in our prayers," but Charles was crestfallen to read, "even though you have not reached the age limit of 20 which is necessary before entering."

Twenty, he thought...I'm only seventeen, and I want to be a monk right after I graduate from high school...That's what I want to do. I am ready now. I don't want to do anything else...

And so, the visits began. Spring breaks, Christmas vacations, a few days here, a week there. For three years Charles waited, visited, observed, learned and deepened his resolution to become a monk. He learned about the monastic life, of course, because whenever he would visit there, the guest master put him to work. Cook and clean up in the kitchen, clean the guest houses, cut the acres of grass, weed the flower gardens, whatever had to be done. In between his chores Charles had many chances to rub elbows with a few monks who ventured down into the guest area. Some, including Brother Paul, would stop, chat, joke and laugh, ask about his life and plans, and some wouldn't. He'd talk with Father Paul, the novice master, and hear him say that waiting was a good thing because it eliminated those who were not sincere and strong in their desire to become monks. Charles would also take Father Paul's advice to enroll in junior college and take philosophy courses until he was twenty and could enter the monastery.

Charles' parents were happy about all this. His mother, June, felt honored and blessed because her son had a vocation to the religious life. She knew nothing about the monastic life, but she was a devout and very active Catholic. As a member of The Altar Guild and the Young Ladies' Institute, she knew many of the church parishioners. She struggled many times to answer their questions about what could possibly be motivating an apparently normal young man to throw his life away in the monastery.

"Is Charles going to become a priest?" the well-intentioned ladies would ask.

"Well, no, I don't think so," she would attempt to explain, "some monks are priests, but the monastery is more a way of life to...to...grow in prayer and...to live on...deeper levels...and Charles tells me that some of the monks are priests and some are not, so they call them brothers."

"Doesn't Charles like girls?" most mothers would eventually get to.

"Yes, he likes girls," June would reassure the worried mothers, "It's just that girls are not the most important thing for him...He just wants to be a monk...they don't allow women inside the actual monastery, the cloister."

"Can he leave the monastery to teach," the practical parishioners would want to know, "or work in hospitals or do something...uh...useful?"

Charles had explained patiently to his mother that for thousands of years certain people had allowed themselves to be called away into what he called "the desert" to seek silence and solitude. She didn't comprehend very well what he had added about living on deeper levels and stripping away the mental idea of the self, but she did understand when he said that monks pray for the world and live a life of compassion, patience and peace. Charles' mother understood praying for others; she was always praying her rosary or offering a Mass for someone else.

June had been Charles' first teacher. She taught her young son not only to pray the standard formalized prayers of the Church like the Our Father, the Hail Mary, the Apostles' Creed, and the Rosary, but also she taught him to follow and understand the Mass, where Catholic dogma explains that the bread and wine are changed into the body and blood of Christ. Of course, Charles' mother also taught him to read, write, draw, cook, sew, and occupy himself creatively when he said he was bored. When he was forty, no longer a monk, and a devoted father a third time, Charles would realize that the most precious lesson she taught him was how the stability and consistency of the family's daily schedule created strong and balanced children. She was always there, welcoming, cooking, maintaining home, hugging, loving.

June also showed Charles how to treat his Down Syndrome brother as if he were a normal boy. Ever since he could remember the white crib appearing in the second bedroom a little after his fifth birthday, Charles had accepted John Scott as his brother, no more and no less. He learned also to understand those who didn't understand his brother. He learned the basic building block of compassion, that each person struggles with some challenge or difficulty, and in that simple fact of life, all people are the same. Charles learned to be patient and sensitive with John, and it was this early challenge and resultant wisdom that allowed the young and then eventually middle-aged man to approach all people as fellow humans, brothers and sisters, sentient and feeling beings.

Charles' father, Carl, not only was not a Catholic, but also he was an unstudied and natural agnostic. He just couldn't fathom how his son would not want to take over the thriving and successful business he had built from the ground up for the last twenty years. He barely managed to graduate from high school after his mother was widowed and remarried. His own carpenter father had slipped off a Minnesota roof to his death, and when he couldn't stop his step-father from physically abusing his mother, he left home to find his own way. From walking the streets hawking paper and pencils during the Depression, to selling typewriter ribbons from a rented store corner in Stockton, California, and finally buying an entire corner building to house his successful typewriter and business supply enterprise, Charles' father was the self-made man who wanted his son to follow similar footsteps. Although he never understood his son's decision, he finally did accept it tacitly. He knew first-hand that a man must find his own way in his own world, and so he never stood in his son's way or tried to dissuade him.

Carl, June, Charles' brother, John, and June's own father,  John (Gramps), later visited the monastery a few months after Charles had become a postulant, and Carl himself saw his son's happiness there. He also met other monks who were from his World War Two generation; they quickly and quietly answered the concerns he had about monks' masculinity.

After his father's death, Charles would not be totally surprised to learn from his mother how happy his father had been when he had eventually left the monastery. The day before he died, he told Charles for the first and last time, "You've been a good son." Charles would forever use that memory of his father's last words to him to ensure that he expressed daily his own love and support for his beloved two sons and two daughters.

"Wuh duh yuh doin' out there, Charles?" his Catholic high school buddies would ask whenever he would disappear behind the north wing of the school building.

"Hey, guys, he's playin' with himself out there, ha-ha..." the crude boys would say.

When he told them he was praying or meditating, they would stop getting on his case, but they didn't understand why he would be praying by himself all the time. Not many understood the silent call to internal spiritual development, and Charles understood that. It was sufficient for him to know and to follow his own insistent call. In his sophomore year he discovered a copy of the Daily Office at Dickerson's Religious Supply downtown, and from that moment until his departure to the monastery seven years later Charles prayed the official Catholic daily prayers seven times a day. He started rising at 3:15 and following the monastic regimen of prayer, study, and silence. He immersed himself in books about contemplation, monastic life, the early Church fathers, especially the mystics such as St. John of the Cross, St. Teresa of Avila, and Meister Eckhart.

At the same time our wanna-be monk moved successfully through high school, continued to ride his bicycle far and wide, and swam into the Pacific whenever his family motored to the coast. In the local junior college, he learned the precision and discipline of creative and essay writing, the intensity and focus of philosophy and logic, the fascination of English and world literature, and the unexpected allure of a beautiful young woman's brown eyes. He spent his time reading, writing papers and poetry, grading essays for his treasured first writing mentors, bespectacled and formal Doctor Briggs and ardent intense Doctor Hunter, riding his Bianchi the several miles to and from classes, and fantasizing from a safe distance about what lay behind that girl's brown eyes. Charles was relieved to have a focus elsewhere. He had no way of knowing then that later in his life, like Goldmund, he would lose and ultimately rediscover himself in the hearts and arms of several strong, beautiful, and fascinating women.

Waiting became Charles' way, his only way: waiting for the next prayer, the next moment of silence, the next class, the next bus to Vina, the next visit to the monastery. By doing what there was to be done at that moment, he filled his waiting with life. Rise before the sun, silence, pray, meditate, breakfast, family, ride to school, read, study, pray, ride home, family, homework and pray, family, ride, dinner, pray, sleep. As his living filled his waiting, Charles became less aware of the waiting as an internal space empty of personal significance, or a period of chronological time marked by no events of any consequence, a challenge to his determination, or even an obstacle to his destiny. Instead, the waiting and doing merged into action called for at the moment; action with intrinsic significance; action that moved Charles' living ahead unperceptively, step-by-step; action more for its own sake than for any imagined or hoped for outcome.

It was just this subtle incremental adjustment during Charles' last year of high school and two years of junior college that caused the time, that to outside observers appeared to be mere waiting, to become for him an opportunity to absorb and create a monastic environment within himself, the monastery in his heart saintly Father Timothy would show him years later during a painful leave-taking. So when Charles' mother, father, and brother finally bid him farewell at the monastery with hugs, kisses and tears, it was as if entering the monastery was just the next thing to do, the next obvious step, not a break from the world, not a leaving, but a continuing stride into life.

"Don't forget to write, dear," Charles' mother reminded him after she kissed him one last time.

Chapter 6: Memos from the Monastery

"Books were written and annotated, systems invented, ancient scrolls collected, new scrolls illuminated, the faith of the people fostered, their credulity smiled upon. Erudition and piety, simplicity and cunning, the wisdom of the testaments and the wisdom of the Greeks, white and black magic—a little of each flourished here; there was room enough for everything, room for meditation and repentance, for gregariousness and the good life." [xviii]
Hermann Hesse
Narcissus and Goldmund

A few job changes have taken place since then. Somewhere about that time I was taken out as cantor and made work coordinator and undermaster of novices. Then about 1978 Thomas asked me to continue those two jobs but to take back the cantor's position as well....not long after... Thomas asked me to replace Regis as cellarer (business manager), which is the job I still have, and which is the main reason it is hard for me to find time to correspond ...In connection with the cellarer's job, I purchased the abbey's first computer back in 1984. We just got a new computer technician, and we're trying to figure out with him the best, cheapest and most efficient way to get multiple simultaneous connections. When that will be achieved is anybody's guess... I'm also work coordinator. The jobs are enjoyable, but very hectic and time-demanding. [xix]
Brother Paul Williams

CHARLES HAD ONE SUITCASE with one change of work clothes, one change of church clothes, and his books. He also had a deep trepidation that his father, Swedish agnostic as he was, would continue not thinking well of his son's decision to abandon the practical world for a religious institution. The first person his father had met during his one and only visit was Brother John, a big John, who happened to mention to the boy's father that he too had been on an aircraft carrier during The War, namely, The Yorktown, coincidently an Essex class carrier, and that there were several other monks at New Clairvaux and at other monasteries who had been in the war.

After a discreet question and answer session with Brother John, Charles' father spent the rest of his good-bye visit smiling at his son. The mother cried, the father patted him on the back, the grandfather who had come along handed him another mother-of-pearl pocketknife, and they all drove out the gate. The young man followed Father Paul, the smiling novice master, from the guest area into the off-limits-to-guests cloister area while the gaunt monk explained patiently to the initiate what he would be encountering the next few days—the schedule, the routines, the bathrooms, the sleeping areas, the barns, the church, the kitchen, how and when to eat—and although the boy listened as if his life depended on everything the master said, the young man was reeling from the subdued joy of being exactly where he had been wanting and struggling and waiting to be for the past seven years.

8:15 PM. Compline

After stacking his books and papers on an unoccupied desk in the monastic ranch novitiate building, and abandoning the box of his few clothes in his cubicle in the dormitory, the now Brother Charles stood uneasily in the choir stall the novice master had led him to, and, as the final evening community prayer began, he tried to imitate the actions and gestures of the monks close around him. Sometimes the community of twenty-seven men was standing, other times bowing, and then often sitting. It was dark in the plain wood-paneled church with only sparse spotlighting over the huge monastic hymnals open in front of the monks. The brothers sang simple, few-note Byzantine-sounding melodies accompanied by a small organ, and with the new-arrival in a daze, Compline suddenly ended with all the monks facing a wooden statue of the Virgin Mary and singing the Salve Regina. The boy was struck by the simple piety and emotion he felt from the monks as they spoke from their hearts to the only female permitted in their lives.

> Hail, holy Queen, Mother of mercy,
> Hail, our life, our sweetness, and our hope.
> To you we cry, the children of Eve;
> To you we send up our sighs,
> Mourning and weeping in this land of tears.
> Turn, then, most gracious advocate,
> Your eyes of mercy toward us;
> Lead us home at last
> And show us the blessed fruit of your womb, Jesus:
> O clement, O loving, O sweet Virgin Mary.

Some monks filed out of the church immediately heading for the dormitory, and some stayed apparently to meditate a little longer. Brother Charles was amused by some monks using a strange variation of sign language as the end of Compline signaled the Grand Silence which ended with Mass the following morning. The dormitory was on the second floor of the old Leland Stanford ranch house built 150 years previous when the world's largest vineyard of 3,500 acres of grapes was producing the finest brandy in the country. The first night Brother Charles lay down on the thin mattress in the 4 x 7 plywood cubicle and wondered if monks, sleeping in such close quarters, dared to pass gas at all, let alone out loud, in the dormitory. He had no choice but to sleep in his clothes because it was so cold in the unheated, uninsulated wooden building.

2:15 AM. Vigils

Unbelievably way too early the next morning the new postulant was jolted awake by someone clanging a deafening hand bell through every inch of dark corridor in the dormitory. He noted 2:15 on his watch, listened another few moments, and decided on the spot that he would haul his still sleeping self off his straw-filled mattress at 2 the next morning to avoid having to listen to the cursed bell. Before the second somnambulistic trial of endurance Brother Charles asked the cellarer for two more heavy muslin sheets and another blanket so he wouldn't shiver all night in the unheated room. The young man's loyal body clock roused him at 2 AM, and he made his careful way down the steep narrow stairs unlit yet before even the bell ringer was awake, down onto the covered cloister walk where the new arrival found his way through the heavy carved wooden swinging double doors into the warm church.

The monastic church was dark except for a few candles here and there, and it smelled welcoming of wood, Tree wax, and frankincense incense. As he stood still in the dark trying to orient himself to where his assigned choir stall was, he sensed a few monks already in church praying or meditating here and there in the limpid darkness. He found his place, knelt and adjusted his newfangled robe and scapular, and began to breathe the name of Jesus, one syllable with each inhalation, and the other with each exhalation. In a few moments a monk in the darkness began turning pages in the huge psalter and then suddenly punctured the meditative silence with a monotone but haunting verse from the Psalms.

> Like the deer that yearns for running streams,
> So my soul is yearning for you, my God.
> My soul is thirsting for God, the God of my life;
> When can I enter and see the face of God.

The other monks and the boy listened in the silence, and then together they intoned the next verse the boy saw was mimeographed on an 8 x 11sheet of paper lit on the shelf along the inside of the choir stall.

> My tears have become my bread,
> By night, by day,
> As I hear it said all the day long:
> "Where is your God?" [xx]

The monks paused at the end of each line, as if each line of prayer was an exhalation of their heart, and when the verse was done, the entire community bowed, and the cantor, alone without the music of the organ, continued with the first line of the next verse, leading the monks in their early morning prayer, the metaphorical vigil of all monks who wait and pray for the arrival of their Lord, whether He be manifested as Christ, Krishna, Buddha, or Allah. The sweet, solitary time between the end of Vigils and the community Mass at six became the boy's predilection.

After a week of experimentation the boy found himself settled in to a balanced and spiritually nourishing schedule. Meditate after Vigils for fifteen minutes in the completely dark church; return to his novitiate desk, turn on the gooseneck lamp, read the Old Testament (*Lectio Divina*), and take meditative notes for an hour or

so; put on his Levi work coat, walk out along the gravel roads that intersect the square mile of monastic land, and let his thoughts dissolve with the smells of the plum orchards and the icy cold waters flowing down from Lassen Peak along Deer Creek where Ishi and his remnant people came down and left their inadvertent arrowheads, pottery shards, and fire ring charcoal; and finally return to one of the long tables in the dimly-lit refectory where he could choose from a buffet-style breakfast—a huge slice of whole wheat monastery bread, peanut butter, non-descript baked eggs, milk, tea, or coffee.

It was this time of early morning that the boy would cherish, feed himself, and revisit many times in his life, and that would culminate in southwestern Idaho, in his sixty-fourth year, rising at 4:15, reading Eknath Easwaran's authoritative and eloquent translations and commentaries on the *Bhagavad Gita*, the *Upanishads*, and the *Dhammapada*, then one of those Hindu scriptures itself, then a half hour of meditation to experience the dimensionless and limitless ground of being in himself, and then prayers and blessings for his family, friends, and all sentient beings both living and dead.

9 AM. Community Mass

Guests always welcomed to the monastery and a few residents of the tiny, vanishing neighboring town of Vina attended the monastic celebration of Mass in the small visitors' room adjacent and open to the church on one side. The six priest-monks concelebrated Mass, and the other twenty or so brother-monks stood around the altar while everyone sang, bowed, sat, stood, took Communion, prayed silently and out loud for their particular intentions, and listened to the Abbot's homily about some aspect of living according to God's will and the Scriptures. Monks the boy would soon recognize as in-charge of cooking, baking, attending to guests, plowing, and setting up the daily work schedule customarily walked out of church as soon as the service ended. Brother Charles lingered to pray for his family, then got up and left with the next group of monks on their way out, and he went to the washroom to change into his work clothes. The Masonite clipboard with morning and afternoon work assignments hung right outside the washroom, and the young man was both apprehensive and excited to read what his tasks would be. In the two years he lived in the monastery, the boy who had never worked on a farm in his life struggled with and finally fulfilled many duties he had never dreamed would define what he always had thought of as the spiritual life.

There were six months of kitchen patrol, peeling bushels of potatoes and carrots, setting the tables with plates and silverware, serving the tables before he sat to eat, washing dishes and the huge pots and pans for the near-thirty people, jeeping the weekly trailer of garbage out to the small dump at the edge of the property, and finally helping Father Vincent in the glorious, yeast-impregnated bakery form and later pull hot loaves of monastery bread from the wide oven. The entire vaulted roof ceiling of the huge two-story brick barn needed to be wire-brushed to remove 150 years of accumulated soot and grime, and Brother Charles lay cramped on his back for three weeks on top of a twenty-foot rickety scaffolding gagging scraping scraping scraping an ancient wire brush with fogged-up goggles protecting his eyes and a suffocating bandana wrapped tightly over his mouth and nose. The young wanna-be monk ran over only two rose bushes while learning how to steer the lawn tractor and negotiate the twists and turns of the two acres of grass around the buildings that needed to be cut every week. He bundled up in the fall when he tractored into the walnut orchards after the harvest and wielded the wicked circular "quick-cut" saw to reach up high into the wide trees and cut out the new green suckers. He took salt tablets all summer when he and Brother Odo pulled the wickedly dangerous 20 foot irrigation pipes off the trailer and nudged then hooked them together into an intricate arrangement that only Brother Odo carried in his head depending on which field they were in.

Always observant, Brother Charles noticed the lack of shelves in the dressing areas by the showers, so the eager postulant volunteered to build them for the monks to stack their one change of clean work clothes. The Abbot, Father Davis, noticed the young man's generosity and scholarship, and asked him to clean and restack all the books in the monastic library, a job he considered to be a chore because of inhaling the characteristic book dust and a delight because he could pause and note on his list for later inspection any book that caught his attention. Father Davis later pointed out his old Underwood typewriter so Charles could help the Abbot catch up on his correspondence that had been piling up.

June 20, 1969

"I work in the kitchen now because the two newest monks work KP every morning. I'm peeling potatoes and onions all the time, setting the dining room for the noon supper, then clean up after. We have twenty-seven monks here now, and after morning work, they're hungry. We eat at 12:15, usually potatoes, some kind of vegetable, fruit from our cannery (usually pears, peaches or apples), great bread from Father Vincent's bakery, milk, or coffee. One of the monks reads something monastic or spiritual during the silent, very formal main meal, have to use sign language in the dining room, also the church, library, dormitory, and from eight at night to nine in the morning. I'll show you some of the signs next time you come up..."

June 29, 1969

"...Checking the clipboard every morning before nine to see what the work assignment is. I've been collecting garbage and taking it out to the monastery dump in an old vintage jeep. Learning how to back up with a trailer. Digging ditches, scraping off old paint and painting on new, cleaning bathrooms this week, last week mopped and waxed the church, learning how to prune walnut trees then collect the brush and burn it in huge mounds, cutting the grass on sit-down mower and trying not to cut down any more small rose bushes. Taking net bags of dirty monastic clothes to the laundry down by Deer Creek is my favorite. Time to look up at the sycamores and Mount Lassen in the distance, listen to the water gurgle by, talk with Brother Adam in his shoe shop next to the laundry about the old days. I am very happy here."

July 14, 1969

"...No work on Sunday. I like to walk around the perimeter of the property, Deer Creek to the north with its lush sycamores and oaks, only dirt and gravel roads to the west and south, the highway to the east. Monks disappear into their own places, very quiet, still without activity, don't know how to find my own balance in the emptiness of the day. I poke around here and there and find little simple surprises, quiet corners. I like to drive the tractors. Pull wagons stacked high with irrigation pipes into the various plum orchards, then connect the pipes in grids that only a few monks know, hook them up to the pumps that suck water from the canals that encircle each field, and turn on the motor. The heat this summer is over 100 degrees most afternoons. Have to take salt tablets to keep going. I take a siesta in the air conditioned dormitory, the only cool place. Also learning how to prune the huge, wide walnut trees using the vicious "Quick Cut" saw. I like to be out alone in the empty orchard with only the trees, squirrels and decisions about which limbs and suckers need to be cut. There's a Mission fig tree by the doors of the tractor barn, and every time I bring in the tractor in the afternoon, I stop a few minutes under the tree and pick off a few luscious ripe figs. I wonder if other monks have done this before me. I hope so... "

July 20, 1969

"...Bells regulate the day here. A monk wakes up before everyone else and walks around the dormitory ringing a huge brass bell to awaken us. After a couple days, I decided to wake up early and get out so I wouldn't have to hear that bell. The church tower bell rings to signal the end of work, the end of the day, and times during the Mass. I still use my watch so I won't arrive late. The church is simple. The monks made it. It's beautiful with light streaming in from the clerestory windows along the top of the walls where they meet the vaulted ceiling. No decoration except a few statues of the Virgin and Joseph. It always smells like furniture wax, candle smoke and incense, a sacred smelling combination. Still getting accustomed to the ceremonies in the church, especially what to do in the choir stalls. Two kinds of bows, sitting, standing and turning at certain times, different people reading. The rhythm of the chanting or singing is beautiful, simple. It reminds me of a line from one of Hart Crane's poems, "Whispers antiphonal in azure swing." I met a monk, Brother Paul, who writes the melodies and does all the copying of the music for the monks. He asked me if I wanted to play my guitar with a couple other monks during Mass. We'll see what happens... "

July 21, 1969

"Last night we watched the TV of the first man setting foot on the surface of the moon. Neil Armstrong and Buzz Aldrin I think were their names; Apollo II was the name of the flight. They let us stay up in the chapter house where there's a TV. Most of the monks wanted to see it, but some of the older monks ignored the historical significance of the event as landing on the moon was not of spiritual significance. We discussed the event a lot, talking about how learning more about the universe can only increase the sense of marvel and respect at the grandeur of God and all of creation. Most monks thought it was a great event to be witnessing, especially when they walked out of the lunar module and set foot on the surface of the moon... "

July 30, 1969

"I fell into one of the irrigation canals the other day. Tried to step across, but forgot that I was wearing robes so my leg wouldn't reach the other side of the concrete canal. I fell in, got wet, skinned my shins, was very embarrassed, but otherwise alright. There's one tree in the entire orchard that has a different kind of plum, and as they ripen some of the monks make a point of walking by to snag the purple beauties. That's where I was going when I almost took a swim in the canal. There's also an old pomegranate tree by the tractor barn that's in full bloom now, pink with little pomegranates starting to form. Someone needs to prune it. I'll ask if I can. We have a family orchard here where the monks grow apples, oranges, grapefruit, pears, and juju fruit. We started canning apples, pears and the juju fruit last week. Usually only about five or six monks in the cannery. It's open all around with the sound and sight of Deer Creek competing with the hot steamy smells of apple and pear sauce and the silence of the monks. The monk in charge of cooking and filling the gallon jars likes cinnamon, so everything smells spicy. My job is cutting up the apples and pears. Blissful work it is. Next door to the cannery is the laundry, tailor shop, walk-in freezer room and Brother Adam's shoe shop. The monastery is like a small town, and it takes a lot of work to keep things going... "

August 5, 1969

"We eat breakfast in the dark refectory. There's always bread, peanut butter, jam, sometimes eggs that look green in the dark, coffee, milk, tea. I sit next to the other monks and nurse my coffee and toast. We all look out through the big windows all around the dining room into the dark. No one talks, and everyone is respectful of everyone else's privacy, their personal space, their silence. I like that a lot. The same with dinner after work. We just come in, get what we want (bread, cheese, tomatoes, lettuce, onions), sit down, eat in silence. I like to make a sandwich with the provolone cheese. Because it's been so hot this summer, they took out the home-made root beer. It's ice cold, and I follow the other monks' lead by drinking a whole quart of it. There's beer too, but I fall asleep if I drink it. I noticed a monk nodding off during Vespers the other day. I guess he had the quart bottle. We get eggs three times a week, and on Sunday we get chicken or fish if we want. I love the food, simple and sufficient."

August 15, 1969

"I have a desk in the novitiate building where the new monks are headquartered. After Matins and breakfast, I go there to read the Old Testament and commentaries on the scriptures. It's dark, and there's a cozy heater, a comfortable and good place to read or study and pray. After work in the afternoon, I'm there again reading the New Testament and commentaries. Everyone respects everyone else here. No rudeness, no noise, respect for each person's space and activity. Started showing some of my books about Zen Buddhism to Father Paul, the novice master. He said there are other monks with interest in Eastern religion too. I guess Thomas Merton introduced it into Trappist monasteries with his writings, so others are curious too. We are going to start a group doing zazen or sitting Zen meditation. We fixed up a little room, and in the afternoon we take turns meditating for thirty minutes in the hot and stuffy little closet. We've been invited sometime soon to a Zen-Christian monastic retreat at a monastery down in the desert mountains in southern California, St. Andrew's Abbey in Valyermo. It's supposed to be an academic exchange and meditation practice using traditional Christian and Zen monastic principles. I'm really excited to talk and meditate with other monks my age. Brother Paul and I talk about this whenever we have a chance. Four of us have been chosen to attend. Can you please bring all my other books under my desk when you come up to visit the next time?"

August 21, 1969

"We finished the prune harvest last week, and to celebrate we went on a picnic to the Plumas National Forest. We spent the day exploring some beautiful areas of the Feather River, a great place for monks, out in the natural beauty and silence of the forest. We got home late (8:30), and it was interesting to see how monks handle having their schedule messed up. A couple guys went into the kitchen and made sandwiches for everyone, some of us hung around after to talk about the trip, and no one made anyone else go to bed or pray or go to church. It reminds me of what Father Paul told me about Saint Benedict. We follow his rule like a lot of Christian monasteries, and he said that before a person can be a good monk, he (or she) has to be a complete human being. I agree that you can't be a person living on the deepest levels of prayer if you aren't a complete person. I guess that's why they discourage people from coming in the monastery instead of encourage them, and don't let them enter until they're twenty. Anyway, it was a great trip. I hope we do that again... "

August 28, 1969

"...The harvest was really a new experience for me. I have never worked on a farm, and the heavy heat of the summer made the work pretty tiring. Brother Paul is in charge of the conveyor belt system, the dipper, they call it, that processes the plums from the field. I started working on the dipper where they bring in large bins of plums they've shaken from the trees in the fields. My first job was to stack the wooden trays as the plums come off the dipper. Then I pulled the stacked trays into the ovens where the plums turned into prunes over a period of a couple days. Then Brother Paul put me on the fork lift, moving bins off the trucks and onto the dumping mechanism of the dipper. It's nerve-wracking work, fast, wet, sometimes enervating with the constant movement of fruit and people and the loud noise of the machinery. During the harvest it always smells like warm sweet fruit. It's the prunes drying in the ovens and the fruit juice that saturates everything. Everywhere else smells like diesel fuel, oil, dirt, and wet bricks. The huge brick barn next to the dipper is from the early days of this ranch when Leland Stanford planted one of the largest vineyards in the country, and he stored the wine in huge barrels in the barn. It smells old and rich in the barn especially when it's full of bins of prunes. Brother Paul (the one who writes the music for the monastery) is in charge of the dipper, and he and I have become friends. He has taught me a lot about how to use the various machines they use in the harvest, the tractors, fork lifts, and the tools to fix everything. He's interested in Eastern religions too, and he knows a lot about Trappist spirituality and the early fathers of the order. He's curious about what I think about life 'outside,' and how I see young people these days adapting to the monastic life."

Chapter 7: Narcissus and Goldmund

"Narcissus knew only too well what a charming golden bird had flown to him. This hermit soon sensed a kindred soul in Goldmund, in spite of their apparent contrasts. Narcissus was dark and spare; Goldmund, a radiant youth. Narcissus was analytical, a thinker; Goldmund, a dreamer with the soul of a child. But something they had in common bridged these contrasts: both were refined; both were different from the other because of obvious gifts and signs; both bore the special mark of fate." [xxi]
Hermann Hesse
Narcissus and Goldmund

Always know that I continue to cherish our friendship and to receive life from it. [xxii]
Brother Paul Williams

AND SO BEGAN MY SPIRITUAL ODYSSEY with Narcissus, my duet with Brother Paul.

I say "duet" because music is a pattern of notes or melodies repeated as variations. The repetition of the variations creates layers of feeling and understanding in the listener's mind and heart. Monastic life is much like music: it follows a schedule, and the routine is the structure that supports the stripping away of self without a person becoming depressed, psychotic, or delusional. There are variations in the schedule—the work and the liturgy change with the seasons, the growth and stages in a monk's psychological and spiritual growth develop in their own time, and the stripping away of false ideas about reality continues relentlessly.

I followed the daily and weekly schedule of life at New Clairvaux Abbey dutifully obeying the times of individual prayer, communal prayer, meals, work, sleep, and spiritual guidance. It was June 1969 and other events were churning around me and my brother monks. The monks huddled in a dark meeting hall staring dumbfounded at a black and white TV as Neil Armstrong stepped onto the surface of the moon. The Woodstock music festival took place in New York with 350,000 in attendance. Demonstrations against the war in Vietnam increased in number and intensity while 250,000 demonstrators marched on Washington in protest. The draft lottery was instituted, but I had received a high number and a ministerial deferment. Radios played what is now considered to be classic music—The Door, Led Zeppelin, Janis Joplin, the Beatles, Jimi Hendrix, Crosby Stills Nash and Young, The Grateful Dead. Richard Nixon became president of the United States. The Altamont Speedway Free Festival turned ugly. The Beatles made their final album together, *Abbey Road*. The race for space intensified with both Russia and the US putting humans in orbit. The first communication was sent through the first computer network, ARPANET. The Public Broadcasting Service (PBS) was created. Charles Manson murdered five people from his cult family. The civil war in Biafra left 3 million people starving. The first eye transplant was made. The Concorde jet was test flown. The first ATM machine was installed in the US. The microprocessor was invented. LSD and marijuana were readily available and cheap on the street. The Pontiac Firebird Trans Am muscle car was introduced to the public. "Sesame Street" debuted on PBS. "Easy Rider," "Midnight Cowboy," and "Butch Cassidy and the Sundance Kid" were among many popular films.

    While the world laughed, danced, got high, took trips on acid, expanded, protested, crashed, and burned, I got up at 2:15 in the morning, chanted the Psalms to Brother Paul's melodies, and immersed myself in the *Old Testament* during early morning free time lit by one desk lamp, and the *New Testament* during afternoon free time lit by sunlight. I walked in the prune and walnut fields to wordlessly witness the sun come up and set. I learned how to prune trees, drive

jeeps and tractors and dump trucks, and do KP twice a day and peel potatoes for thirty men. I set out and picked up 20 foot irrigation pipes, helped core and can gallon jar after gallon jar of pears or juju fruit, and cleaned the community bathrooms and the church. I took salt tablets during the 100 degree heat of the prune and walnut harvests, and I put on every layer of clothing I had to ward off the freezing ice of the winter.

And Brother Paul and I worked together on the prune dipper. I was twenty, and Brother Paul forty. Here was a man who worked hard taking care of many of the critical jobs that kept the monastery going—writing the music for the liturgy, ordering the day-to-day supplies for the community, taking care of the irrigation and managing the water supplies from the surrounding counties, attending agriculture and irrigation meetings around the county, and riding roughshod on the dipper during the prune harvest.

Yet here was a man who was looking for the same elusive thing as I was—how to best live on the deepest levels of life. He had chosen New Clairvaux Abbey as his dojo, his battleground, his arena. And I thought the monastery was the best place to stand my ground too. Before work in the morning or after work in the afternoon we would often meet in his small office in the corner of the huge brick barns where 8 foot square bins of prunes were stored along with all the farm machinery. The barn smelled of oil, diesel, and dirt, but it was cool in the summer, and doves and pigeons made their homes in the high soot-covered ceilings.

Brother Paul's office contained a large, old-fashioned drafting table where he kept his papers and books, and a small electric organ where he composed the melodies for the community liturgies. In the dark mornings the warm light from the arched windows punctured the brick walls with a welcome glow, and I knew it meant that Paul was there. I lugged in books I had brought from home, Hesse, of course—*Siddhartha, Demian, The Glass Bead Game, Narcissus and Goldmund*; bad translations of *The Bhagavad Gita, The Upanishads, The Yoga Sutras* of Patanjali, the poetry of Hart Crane, Walt Whitman, T.S. Eliot, e.e.cummings, haiku by the Japanese masters. We mulled over out loud again and again in a different key, at a different rhythm, in variation upon variation, how God was inherent in all art, how words managed—usually barely, sometimes magnificently—to communicate the Ground of Being we sought and sometimes experienced in and out of the monastery.

> "He thought that fear of death was perhaps the root of all art, perhaps also of all things of the mind. We fear death, we shudder at life's instability, we grieve to see the flowers wild again and again, and the leaves fall, and in our hearts we know that we, too, are transitory and will soon disappear. When artists create pictures and thinkers search for laws and formulate thoughts, it is in order to salvage something from the great dance of death, to make something that lasts longer than we do." xxiii

We began not only to discuss what the words pointed to—their denotation and connotation, but also to lament, but more often delight, in the fact that words, our words, could never communicate satisfactorily that experience of God, the Ground of Being, we both sought and experienced. Years later we wrote series of letters to each other struggling moment-to-moment with the challenge of speaking about an experience that is essentially not verbal, and Brother Paul often used the term we invented—MU—to mean "No words can say it."

> *I enjoyed your stumbling efforts to convey the shift in your perception of reality. Best to lapse into our old friend MU. 'Be still and know that I am God.' The reverberations of that are infinite. Words pointing into the unknown and the unknowable. The mysterium. Filling, humbling, very private (yet at the heart of humankind), productive, some kind of rich secret fruit, a harvest. But as you say, don't ramble on, or you diminish the reality... Be still. Only by being still will you know. And*

you can't talk about it because when you start talking about it, you quit knowing. All this makes immense sense, yet it makes no sense at all. So better to be still and just let it be. xxiv

Summer time at the monastery brings the ripening, not only of friendships, but also of fruit trees in the family orchard—summer pears, apples, oranges, grapefruit, juju fruit, and every monk looks forward to the week or so when the canning of that bounty comes together. In an isolated corner of the property, where Deer Creek gurgles over gravel beds and sings through a small stand of aspens and birch trees, the monks had constructed the cannery, a small concrete block building of two sections about 16 by 32 feet. One half is roofed concrete wall four feet high with screened windows all around. Blissful monks stand quietly around stainless steel tables there peeling, quartering, and paring fruit brought in by bucketsful during the morning and afternoon work sessions. The other half of the cannery has a large window in each of the full-size walls around which hang narrow benches and shelves heaped with gallon jars, canning lids and rings, large wooden spoons, bags of sugar, and piles of cinnamon sticks and whole cloves.

In the center of the unlit room—a ravenous object of worship that steams and hisses its satisfaction—the huge, round, propane-fueled steam kettle sits belching and whistling from its pressure release valve, appeased for the moment by the load of twelve gallon jars of sweet fruit boiling away inside its stainless steel confinement. Monks attending to the canning are stuffing cut fruit into jars, inserting whole cinnamon sticks between the layers of fruit, making and pouring sugar syrup into the filled jars, then screwing the lids and rings on each jar. Every fifteen minutes or so, Brother Adam nods to Brother Seraphim to open the pressure cooker, and the peeling, quartering, and paring monks can hear the hissing of the steam release, so that the small building fills with a cloud of cinnamon-apple scented vapor. Every monk knows that when the freezing cold winter of Northern California arrives, and the trees in all the Sacramento Valley are skeletal shadows, these very jars of delectable fruit will be opened and served for dessert at the mid-day meal. I looked forward to spooning the Bartlett pears I was peeling into my bowl, and ladling the fragrant syrup over the sections of luscious fruit.

To signal the end of work every morning and afternoon, Brother Pierre would pull the rope down slowly with both hands then release it suddenly, and the huge Spanish bell in the church tower exploded with an urgency that carried everywhere in the monastic grounds and out past Vina to old Highway 99 where a bus stop lets monastery guests off by the sign with the arrow and the word, "Monastery." I had been repairing one of the thousands of damaged wooden-slatted trays used to stack and dry the plums to be harvested. I put down my hammer, listened to the sweet "Come on Back Home" sound of the bell, then got on my dog-eared, balloon-tired cruiser and pedaled back slowly to the washroom. I cleaned up, put my robe over my work clothes, and arrived in the church with my brothers for the midday common prayer, and then afterwards the day's one formal meal eaten in common.

It's difficult to let one's work drop at the sound of a bell, regardless if the work is inspired or not, but that is the centuries-old structure of the Trappist day—work and prayer, and both are sacred. After a few minutes when the monks arrive one-by-one in church and collect their thoughts, the cantor starts to play the first few bars of organ music while the monks find the mimeographed sheet with the daily prayers from the psalms and other scriptures related to the ecclesiastical time of year. There is the usual singing of simple melodic lines put to the text of the daily readings of the Church. Each day I sang a little louder as I learned the subtleties of the antiphonal responses.

I had been at the monastery more than four months doing KP when a new postulant, Brother Alex, mercifully took my place in the ever-busy kitchen, so I was able to file into the kitchen with the rest of the community rather than prepping and waiting in the refectory for the other monks' arrival. I found my place at the long, narrow wooden table with the others, waited for the elderly, arthritic and slow-to-arrive monks, bowed for the Abbot's blessing, and then sat on the wooden bench. Monks passed bowls of potatoes, string beans, lentils, and plates with bread and butter, then the pitchers of milk. Very soon I noticed the pattern of fish and fowl served on

Sundays only, and eventually it mattered not what I ate given the fact there was always enough. While one of the brothers read out loud from a commentary on the scriptures or a psychological treatise on spiritual development, the monks listened politely and stared out the windows around the refectory looking for some part of their lives still unidentified, not yet located, or lost on their journey. I made the sign for milk, poured more into my big stainless steel mug, and passed it on down the table. Brother Alex came around with huge bowls of watermelon slices for each table, and most monks limited themselves to two slices, so I copied their table etiquette.

The Abbot stood slowly to signal that the meal had finished, the community intoned the Lord's Prayer, and as monks filed out while putting their dirty dishes into the grey plastic bins, Brother Regis, in charge of all work at the monastery, tapped me on the forearm and made the sign that I should come to the work office. I signed, "Now?" wondering if I would have time to take a 30 minute siesta in the air conditioned dormitory before going out for the afternoon work. The Cellarer nodded his head once, and I suspected there was to be some kind of change in work assignments; there was. Summer brings the two main harvests—first the prune in the early part of the summer, then the walnut towards the end. Every monk had been working the extra hour until 5 getting ready for the plum harvest, the biggest moneymaker for the self-sufficient community.

The Cellarer had come around early on that day to verify that I had nearly finished repairing the damaged wooden slats on the trays used to dry the plums, and I was not surprised when Brother Regis began to speak.

"So, Brother Charles, how is monastery life treating you?"

"So far, Brother, everything is moving along just perfect, although everything is new to me, or course."

"You'll get used to it little by little, everyone does...I hear from the Abbot that you are a good and conscientious worker," the middle-aged, balding monk smiled and raised his eyebrows.

"Well, I try to do my best, Brother, that's all, and I just ask someone if I don't know exactly what to do," I nodded modestly.

"That's good, just the way it should be, Brother Charles...and that's the exact reason I want you to start working with Brother Paul on the dipper... the plums will be ready this coming Monday or Tuesday, so we'll start shaking then...Have you ever worked on a harvest, Brother?"

"No, I haven't, I haven't, but I'm ready to learn."

"I'm going to put you to work with Brother Paul, he's a good teacher, and you and he will be working together on the dipper."

"The dipper?"

Brother Regis took a few minutes to outline for me the entire progression of the plum harvest. First, the tractors approach the plum trees, grab the tree trunks with their giant plier-like pincers, and then they unfold two canvas wings onto the ground on both sides of the trees. The pincer violently shakes each tree so the sustained vibration causes the ripe fruit to fall onto the unfolded canvas wings which then fold up and tip the fruit into giant six foot wooden bins. The bins are trucked back into the monastery where the fruit is gently poured onto the receiving end of the dipper. The fruit is cleaned, stacked on trays, dehydrated in the monastery ovens, and then stored in huge bins in the barn for delivery to Sunsweet in Corning.

"So once a bin is dumped into this part of the dipper," Brother Paul pointed out later that afternoon after Regis had taken me to Paul's office to introduce us to each other, "the fruit is washed, then the leaves and stems are removed...here, and the fruit goes along the conveyer belt here, where we cull out any bad looking fruit, and then the prunes are deposited on these trays here..."

Brother Paul pointed out the Rube Goldberg contraption that lowered and stacked a new tray on top of the rising column of full trays, the knob to regulate the speed of the entire dipper, the kill-switch in case the dipper needed to be stopped for some reason, and the rusted steel track curving from the stacking area around and into the huge dehydrating ovens under the barn next to the dipper. Very quickly I learned to listen to my instincts about shutting down the dipper. One tray swollen by water or out of square can jamb the entire stacking mechanism, fall askew onto the previous tray, spilling its contents of two-hundred or so plums all over the work area where I would have to hurry and pick up the ones I wasn't already stepping on. More than one time, when a tall column of 30 or so trays was ready to be pulled out quickly to make way for a new square, angle-iron, four-wheeled under-carriage to stack the next column of trays on; I would pull a little too authoritatively, and the entire column of trays full of plums would tilt and fall over, cascading plums and wooden trays over the entire area. I wondered more than once if I was incompetent or if these mishaps were characteristic of a fruit harvest.

    Every day or so after work Brother Paul and I picked out a phrase, a word, a concept from one of my books or his, added a bass line from the *New* or *Old Testament*, and played out the cycle of ideas over the relentless racket of The Dipper. It was Brother Paul, who, during the June days of the 1969 prune harvest, had been delegated to prepare and then love and care for The Dipper. In spite of his calling to compassion and love, he detested the machine. Only because he had answered willingly the call to monastic obedience did he good-naturedly accept this preeminent call to The Dipper. He became its master.

    The Dipper was a marvelous machine, not quite up to the complex or humorous standards of Rube Goldberg, but complicated and interconnected all the same, demanding attention and fine-tuning, pushing and nudging, oiling and greasing, replacement parts hand-fabricated on the spot, and tender, loving care. It was an intricate and complicated system of conveyer belts, chains and pulleys, vats, hinges, towers, wires, and pneumatic hoses that every five minutes received into its maw an eight foot square wooden bin full of ripe prune plums straight from the monastery fields. It washed the plums, removed the stems and leaves, allowed sharp-eyes monks to cull the rejects by hand, deposited approximately two-hundred plums on three foot square wooden trays, stacked one-by-one thirty of these dripping wet and plum laden trays often imprecisely on top of a four wheeled steel dolly, buzzed annoyingly to signal a waiting monk to lug the ponderous tower of trays and plums out of the stacking jig, and continued implacably to deposit plum-laden trays on what hopefully was another perfectly positioned steel dolly that that same frazzled monk had hustled in place of the tower of trays he had just removed. Any monk could stop the relentless machine with the push of one of many strategically located red buttons. Only a mechanical breakdown or a toppling stack of prunes tumbling everywhere would move anyone to take on such a responsibility.

It was in the din and hubbub of this same detestable Dipper that I became initiated during my first (and only) summer harvest into the world of monastic labor. The August harvest coincided with hundred degree plus temperatures in the Sacramento Valley, and many probationary monks could not tolerate either the six to eight hour work days or the blistering and enervating heat. Many vocations to the monastery were dissolved and reduced to tears under the mute toil of the plum and later the walnut harvests. It was during that sweating, pushing, pulling, driving, lugging, wiping, stacking, fixing and waiting that Brother Paul and I met and discovered an association we had no way of knowing would eventually come to signal the beginning and the end of our personal and intimate world.

> "But the love that bound him to his friend and their habit of spending much time together had not been fruitless. In spite of the vast differences of their characters, each had learned much from the other. Beside the language of reason, a language of the soul had gradually come into being between them; it was as if, branching off the main street, there are many small, almost secret lanes. Gradually the imaginative power of Goldmund's soul had tracked such paths into Narcissus's thoughts and expressions, making him understand—and sympathize with—many of Goldmund's perceptions and feeling, without need for words. New links from soul to soul developed in the warm glow of love; words came later." [xxv]

I had never met a man like Brother Paul. He was living at the deep level of perception and awareness I sought. He was articulate, literary, and musical, proclivities I had relished and enjoyed as a young man. He was a hard worker willing to take on any task whether mundane or challenging. He had a witty sense of humor that transcended beliefs and dogma. He was intelligent and able to perceive patterns both subtle and three-dimensional. He was a solitary contemplative monk and at the same time a member of the monastic community and countywide farming organizations. He was able to love everything and everyone with a passion I had yet to experience or understand. And finally, he was a man who had both masculine and feminine energies at work throughout all his faculties. It would be years until I really understood his unseen struggle as a celibate monk to accept, manage, and express his love for both men and women.

 I have never met a man like Brother Paul since then.
 I mourn that fact every day.
 Where are the men like him in this world?

Chapter 8: Leaving

"He saw Goldmund fed from secret sources to which he, himself, had no access; he had been able to further their growth, but had no part in them. Though he was glad to see his friend freeing himself of his guidance, he also felt sad. He saw that this friendship, which had meant so much to him, was nearing its end. He still knew more about Goldmund than Goldmund knew about himself. Goldmund had rediscovered his soul and was ready to follow its call, but he did not know where it would lead him. Narcissus knew this and felt powerless; his favorite's path led to regions in which he himself would never travel." [xxvi]

Hermann Hesse
Narcissus and Goldmund

It may sound corny, but I have carried you in my heart all these years, Chas, and often the thought of you would bubble up into consciousness, and I would wonder where you were, who you were with, what you were doing. [xxvii]

Brother Paul Williams

"BROTHER CHARLES, THE ABBOT AND I THINK IT BEST if you return to school and finish your education at a university."

The novice master, Father Paul, looked me in the eye, and I knew my immediate future was not to be as I had imagined. The prune harvest had ended, and monks had finished cleaning up from the walnut harvest in mid-August. I was cozy and content in my mostly silent niche of study, prayer, meditation, work, and my budding and quickly deepening friendship with Brother Paul.

In my mind I said, *I'm not going to leave this place I've been waiting to be in for the past six years when I just got here*, but my mouth said, "Alright, Father Paul. When do you think I should return to school?"

"Right away."

Within five days the gears of change were grinding quickly inside the monastic machine that wanted intelligent and educated monks ready to live a spiritual life in a modern, post-Vatican II world, ready to be able to explain clearly to the public what the monastic life was all about, ready to make monasticism a strong force for good in the world. I was enrolled in The University of California at Santa Cruz where I would live in my parents' Aptos summer house close to the campus.

On my last day at the abbey I received a note indicating that frail and saintly Father Timothy wanted to meet with me after the afternoon work. We met on the grass under a huge arching elm tree. He asked what I would be studying, where I would be staying, how I felt about leaving. The then-only hermit in the community, he had bicycled in from his little hut located in a wooded part of the monastery to see me off. I had never spoken with him directly for more than a greeting or a nod in passing, so I had no idea why he wanted to speak with me. I never could have predicted that the few simple words he would say to me would be burned in my mind for as long as I lived.

"I really don't want to leave, Father," I proceeded to explain my predicament to this man I didn't know and whose mist-clouded eyes saw into worlds I had never experienced, "but Father Paul and the Abbot think it best that I finish my studies, so that's fine with me..." I finished with obvious half-hearted enthusiasm. The saintly monk smiled, reached under his black scapular, and pulled out a holy card, one of the ubiquitous tokens of thoughtfulness, care, and blessing that monks give people on various occasions. He handed me the card and waited while I read out loud the elaborate printing on the front.

"God is Love and he who abides in love abides in God and God in him. St. John"

He nodded and smiled towards the card, and I turned it over to read the tiny sparse handwritten message the holy man had written to me on the last day of the year.

"With your mind in the hands of your heart BE before God—This is to be a monk, a man of prayer, a wise man, and in His Light you will penetrate to the meaning of all things"

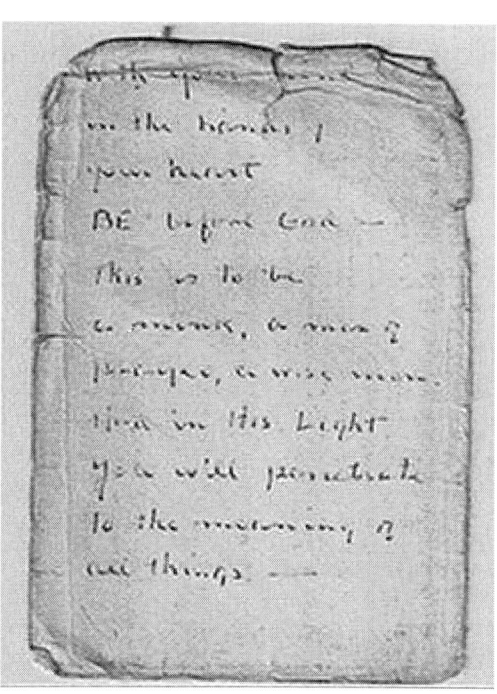

He beamed a wise and compassionate smile and counseled, "You'll be leaving this place, that's true, Brother Charles, but you will be carrying the monastery with you in your heart." The devout, childlike man stepped a bit closer to me and said one final time and forever, "You carry your monastery in your heart, Brother Charles, in your heart."

"Thank you, Father, I will remember that," I said simply as we embraced as men, monks, seekers of the Face of God. I remember his words to this day as I read those words that I just transcribed from fading ink on the card in my furrowed hands.

Very early the next morning after Vigils and then Mass, I packed my few possessions thinking I would be back, *Yes, I will be back soon*, and I walked slowly through the darkness to the abbey ranch office to say good-bye to the first person I ever loved. Brother Paul was waiting for me. Without many words from either of us, we embraced like the dearest of old friends meeting after many years, like forlorn friends who lost someone, like timeworn friends who still love each other. We embraced wordlessly for an hour in the warm low light of Brother Paul's office. We cried, we laughed. We spoke of my return the following summer. We felt the surprise and the intensity of our love for each other.

> "Listen, Goldmund! Our friendship has been good; it had a goal and the goal has been reached; you've been awakened. I would like it not to be over; I would like it to renew itself once more, renew itself again and again, and lead to new goals. For the moment there is no goal. Yours is uncertain, I can neither lead you nor accompany you." [xxviii]

> *It would be nice to hold you and be held by you again. Our long embrace of many years ago remains for me an ever fresh and pregnant symbol of a cherished friendship. Your January letter was the first time you characterized our friendship as an "explosion of passion and emotion and love." Although I may be Narcissus, I like it when you put it that way. I was pleasantly surprised to learn that it was your first experience of passionate love and that you found it a little scary but powerful. You were in your early 20s at the time, but I was already in my late 30s... However, it was the only time I've ever embraced anyone quietly for over an hour. I didn't find that scary, but I did find it archetypal. Some way or another, I felt we were at the guts of how it is to be human.* [xxix]

It was an odd desolate trip later that day driving from Vina to my family home in Stockton. I sat in the back seat of the monastery sedan next to gaunt Father Paul, the novice master, and in the front seat big World War II Brother John drove us north along Interstate Highway 5, while in the front passenger seat incredibly enough sat the abbot himself, refined and generous Father Bernard. That night the four men in black and white habits sat close around my mother June's green Formica kitchen table next to my father in his brown suit and red bowtie, me in my white postulant's habit, and my ever-curious Down Syndrome brother, John, while my solicitous mother served her typical spread—baked chicken, zucchini casserole, salad, and apple pie. I enjoyed seeing them all dig in with un-monkish gusto and relish my dear mother's wonderful cooking.

Before leaving the abbot snuck out to the car and brought in from the trunk something I did not know about. After my mother passed away, I found it on the wall of her home, and it hangs now in the vestibule of our house—the meticulously embroidered silk picture of the traditional "Brave Tiger," symbolizing good fortune. I am sure the good abbot acquired the beautiful memento on his journey to Hong Kong to sponsor New Clairvaux's first daughter house, Our Lady of Joy Abbey, in Lantao. Father Bernard's gift represents so simply the refinement, learning, open-mindedness, cultural awareness, and generosity that characterizes Trappist monks and nuns the world over. The gracious giving and receiving of the gift was the signal for all to rise; the monks had miles to go before they slept.

They drove the next few hours to the Zen Center in San Francisco, and *I* slept the next twelve hours in my own sweet bed in my first home. To the university later. The monks' destination mirrored and fueled my own desire to delve deeper into my own experience of mediation and into my intellectual clarity about religion. I set up a plan of independent study in Religious Studies at

The University of California at Santa Cruz, and while there I soon came under the powerful influence of two great men, contemporary sages they are, men who became my teachers and mentors, Doctor Noel King and Doctor Lewis Keizer. xxx

Each quarter I would sign up for as many of Doctor King's classes as I could—seminars, lectures, and colloquia with Doctor King about African traditional philosophy and religions, the influences of Islam in Africa, Sufism, topics of faith, culture, and revelation with books by Buber, Niebuhr, and Barth. Yet it was the weekly meetings in Dr. King's apartment that taught me more than what I learned from his exhaustive and fascinating book list. A Sikh/Indian grandfather, an obvious Hindu manifestation of Lord Vishnu, his rugged beaming face surrounded by a halo of glowing grey hair and beard, all these incarnations met you at the door with welcoming love from his heart and an embrace. Students of all descriptions wanted to take his classes and to be in his warm on-campus home. I learned from Doctor King that spirituality is embodied in people; The Eternal Self is manifested in all sentient beings; we see ourselves in all, and all in ourselves, to paraphrase *The Bhagavad Gita*. xxxi

Then Doctor Lewis Keizer introduced me to two critical concepts in the development of my own understanding of the nature of religion, belief, and mysticism. I bought my Koine Greek *New Testament* and dictionary, and began my personal discovery of scriptural exegesis—the examination of words and phrases, their linguistic and historical significance, the following of a story or teaching cores inoculated by one scripture to another, the identification of the earliest and most authentic scriptures by following the use and misuse of certain words and phrases, and in that complex process the delving into the intended linguistic and so spiritual significance of the text.

This short erudite man with trimmed beard, always dressed in a suit, a tie, and vest, a bishop-at-large, and a cool jazz trumpeter, also laid out for the cramped minds in his classes the deep and wide panorama of the Intertestamental Period where and when Judaism gave birth to Christianity, a painful and protracted birth with complications and interventions. Religions emerge from historical times and places via the mediation of a divine avatar, and in Doctor Keizer's world, it was Jesus who is the Christ.

Doctor Keizer endeared me eternally when I arrived at the door of his apartment on the university campus eager and ready to turn in my Senior Thesis for graduation. I knocked, waited, knocked again, waited, and since I had arrived at the agreed upon time, I decided to wait and see if he came eventually to the door. I don't remember if he opened the door wrapped in a towel or not, but it was clear that the body of work he was attending to in his apartment had nothing to do with scriptural exegesis. He took my Thesis not the least bit chagrined, we parted, I passed his class, and I graduated with Honors in Religious Studies.

Doctor Keizer certainly helped me add another descriptor to my growing definition of a spiritual man. Doctor King has since returned to the Divine Unmanifested Self, and at this writing Doctor Keizer continues to witness and minister to the manifestations and revelations of the Self in everything. They remain spiritual fathers for thousands of fortunate seekers who are blessed forever for having been in their classes and come to know them as human beings. They both represent the best that a man could be. May they be blessed forever. They are.

During my two academic years at UCSC I was led to the classical eastern religions' scriptures—the *Upanishads*, the *Yoga Sutras* by Patanjali, and *The Bhagavad Gita*, in addition to every book about Zen Buddhism I could find in the inviting and cozy university library or Santa Cruz city bookstores. Surfing at Pleasure Point, classes on nutrition, the now-legendary open-to-all vegetarian dinners at Alan Chadwick's prolific garden served on huge wooden tables by sweet and unrestrained barefoot coeds, and 100% whole wheat bread made my hiatus from the monastery easier to tolerate. Several times I wore my white postulant's habit with scapular and hood to my classes. It is fascinating how we human beings take on new external habits (unintentional pun) that eventually or not become internalized so that appearances no longer matter at all.

Many western monks have found that they have arrived in the metaphorical East without having set out in that direction at the beginning of their spiritual journey. Dom Bede Griffiths and Master

Thomas Merton are two exemplary western monks whose lives became transformed by their understanding, study, and eventual immersion in Buddhism and Hinduism respectively. Their personal exchanges with Eastern monks and monasticism paved the way and set the example for other monks and monastic orders to follow. When I returned to the abbey at the end of my first year of university classes, I brought with me a deep interest in Zen meditation, both sitting meditation (zazen) and walking meditation (kin-kin). Brother Paul became infected with the intellectual intrigue of the "not-this, not-that" philosophy of stripping away intellectual limitations of attributing certain characteristics to God and of the insidious trap of thinking of Reality in dualistic terms.

Father Paul, the open-minded novice master, agreed to sponsor a small group of younger monks who wanted to do zazen meditation, and he quietly arranged to set up a small room available by appointment only for individual zazen meditation sessions. A few times that summer the monastery van motored several monks to the Zen Center in San Francisco where we mediated, ate, and talked "emptiness" with Zen monks; and to St. Andrew's Abbey Benedictine monastery in the California desert town of Valyermo where young Benedictine monks there collaborated with us in meditating and having Venn Diagram discussions about Christianity and Zen Buddhism.

During that summer's harvest I learned to drive the monastery farm's World War Two Jeep, wrestled with an old John Deere tractor, and avoided driving mishaps with a veteran dump truck bristling with several oddly shaped floor shift levers I never quite understood or used. I pruned more walnut trees, plucked ripe Mission figs from low-hanging branches, canned more apples and pears, and worked with Brother Paul on the unrelenting dipper. Give two friends the opportunity to work together closely on a daily basis; give them time to pray, meditate, and walk in the fields together without saying a word, or sit in a cozy office to discuss the implications of being a human man striving to live on the deepest levels in God; and given the reality that the two friends would have very little time to discover the urgency, depth, and importance of their friendship—and you have the ingredients for understanding, respect, and love to send down roots deep into those two men's unsuspecting hearts and minds.

Every day, and sometimes not, we met in the warm glow of the tiny abbey ranch office in the late afternoon summer heat, or we walked out into the morning or afternoon fields along one of the  many north-south-east-west dirt and gravel roads, or in the spring thaw we ambled along the steep banks of Deer Creek rushing impatiently down from Lassen, or in the evening light we aimed our footsteps out towards the far end of the property to taste the tiny wild plums glistening and bursting with tangy juice along the natural drainage canals there. We spoke of life, our own lives, our histories of love and learning, how the mystery of sex had a place in spirituality, our struggle to love God while being human, being men, and the mystery of The Other. We talked of the monastic vows of stability and chastity that on the surface limit personal growth but that in the long run channel one's energies in the direction one wants to travel.

And we felt the limits of our words again, so articulate at first, so compelling between the mind of one friend and another, so useful to explain how one feels about one's life and journey, words so wonderful and rich in themselves as music, poetry or prayer. We arrived again at Mu, where words no longer suffice to communicate the deepening essence of experience. Over that summer Paul and I were astounded to rediscover more and deeper layers in Hesse's novel, *Narcissus and Goldmund*, depicting so perfectly the external and internal history (and little did we know, the future) of our relationship as monks and men.

When I left mid-harvest to return to UCSC for my second and final year of studies before getting a degree, it was with the unspoken assumption that I would be returning to the monastery to become a novice and then professed monk, living and working in that community of prayer for the rest of my life. I felt odd to leave the monastery again, leave my Narcissus, leave my well-planned out life to return to finish my studies at the university. Dutifully I said my good-byes to Brother Paul promising to write and excited projections about my final return to the monastery when I graduated from UC at Santa Cruz. Neither of us had any inkling that my return would be under much different circumstances twenty-two Goldmund-like years later, full of remorse, gratitude, and love.

> "It sounded like a farewell; it was indeed a foretaste of farewell. Goldmund stood looking at his friend, the determined face, the goal-directed eyes; he had the unmistakable feeling that they were no longer brothers, colleagues, equals; their ways had already parted. The man before him was not a dreamer; he was not waiting for fate to call to him. He was a monk who had pledged his life, who belonged to an established order, to duty; he was a servant, a soldier of religion, of the church, of the mind. Goldmund now knew he did not belong here; this had become clear to him today. He had no home; an unknown world awaited him." [xxxii] "Oh, now well Narcissus had recognized all this long ago; how right he had been!" [xxxiii]

Your departure from Vina reminds me of something I may or may not have told you before. Having been here some 43 years now, I've been through many departures—some much more painful than others, depending on how close we have been. The latest was just last February, and the experience confirmed what I've felt for a long time now: the hardest part of monastic life is having to part with friends whom you hoped would be your brothers for life. [xxxiv]

Chapter 9: Wanderer

"I am superior to you only in one point: I'm awake, whereas you are only half awake, or completely asleep sometimes. I call a man awake who knows in his conscious reason his innermost *unreasonable* force, drives, and weaknesses and knows how to deal with them. For you to learn that about yourself is the potential reason for your having met me. In your case, mind and nature, consciousness and dream world lie very far apart." [xxxv]
Hermann Hesse
Narcissus and Goldmund

First of all I want very much to ask you about yourself. You wrote virtually nothing, which was understandable since you had no idea if I would even receive the letter...whatever kind of face you wear, dear friend, I love you as you are... The years...How many of them are there now? [xxxvi]
Brother Paul Williams

AT THE UNIVERSITY ONE LAST TIME I read and studied more the scriptures of the world religions, particularly from Buddhism and Hinduism, continued learning Greek to read the *New Testament* in its original language, and immersed myself in the "unknowing" Western mystics such as Meister Eckhart, Nicolas of Cusa, Teresa of Avila, Therese Lisieux, and the master of the Dark Night of the Soul and Spirit, John of the Cross. I bussed back to the monastery during the Christmas break; submerged myself in the daily cycle of prayer and work; became more confident with farm machinery and the cycles of planting and harvesting; and all the while shared the silence of the early morning, the gravel roads through the prune and walnut fields, and the coziness of the abbey ranch office with Brother Paul, my dear Narcissus.

Without knowing it, without wanting it, or without being able to avoid it, we slowly discovered each previously hidden dimension of ourselves being fitted into the invisible twin archetypes Hermann Hesse so astutely and eloquently embodied in the ascetic and committed monk, Narcissus, and his dear friend, the worldly and passionate Goldmund. It was our sweet myopia often lamented as characteristic of love that prevented us from heeding with caution the last part of Hesse's tale. Goldmund would leave his monastery and his Narcissus, and I would too soon leave my monastery and my Brother Paul.

I returned to the university mid-harvest in August, and eight months later, ironically, in Santa Cruz, that is, Holy Cross, on April 19, Good Friday of Easter week 1971, the day Christians celebrate the suffering and crucifixion of Jesus and His pardon of the thief crucified next to him; I sat and paced and agonized the entire day alone and mute over another clear and insistent inner voice enjoining me to not return to the monastery, but instead to follow my invisible, insistent, and always true compass into the world of Goldmund. I had repeated to myself like a new mantra that The Rule of Saint Bernard that ordered the lives of Trappist monks said wisely that one had to be a full human being before one could be a genuine monk. I told myself that again and again. Again and again. And after all, Father Timothy had assured me that I could carry my monastery in my heart. I have always known that he was right. I know it even more now.

It's not at all odd that we humans mark the location of our internal time at introspective moments by sounding a few deep events in our past to send back an echo that vibrates our hearts and minds in the perfect key to which we have carefully tuned ourselves. Leaving the monastery—my painful decision, the report I sent the abbot and novice master, the strained letter I sent Brother Paul, the chaos over what I would do with my life after the monastery, the first time I went back to visit Brother Paul twenty-two years later—that one judgment is one of the most painful yet crucial decisions I have ever made in my life.

What would I do, where would I go, what direction would I take, would I ever love anyone else as I loved Brother Paul? What would happen to the Narcissus and Goldmund story he and I had begun to embody? I did not see the archetypical forces at work in me to know any more than the starkly simple fact that I was leaving everything I had ever wanted and loved. And I was leaving Paul.

"Would he succeed in saving a few scraps of this inner world and making it visible to others? Or would things just go on the same way: new towns, new landscapes, new women, new experiences, new images, piled one on the other, experiences from which he gleaned nothing but a restless, torturous as well as beautiful overflowing of the heart?" [xxxvii]

"Now I see that it was really so, that you really do love me. But I have always loved you, Narcissus. Half of my life was spent courting you. I knew that you, too, were fond of me, but I never dared hope that you would tell me some day, you're such a proud man. You give me your love in this moment when I have nothing left, when wandering and freedom, world and women have abandoned me. I accept it and I thank you for it." [xxxviii]

After I left New Clairvaux Abbey and Brother Paul, I wandered for 15 timeless years inside my heart and mind. I moved from city to city around beautiful and mythic Monterey Bay in a myopic and iterative scavenger hunt for companionship, love, and completion. I loved many different people. I was very alone. I made things, musical instruments—a sitar and dulcimer, mobiles from balsa wood and rice paper, anything to manifest my spirit. I wrote pages and pages of poetry. I felt desire and ecstasy. I felt emptiness and longing. I needed to know others' inner worlds. I sought unity and wholeness in loving and creating as I had with Brother Paul.

I moved to Salinas, California, where I became a teacher in the Teacher Corps; where I learned about English as a Second Language students from Mexico working twelve hours in the lettuce and broccoli fields; where I went to farm labor camps, set up a blackboard, and tried to teach tired campesinos with cans of Coors in their hands, "My name is Juan…I live in Salinas;" where I screwed a black light into the ceiling fixture of my bedroom in the three-bedroom house I shared with two other odd-ball guys learning how to be teachers; before I drove to San Francisco on window pane acid in Chuck's faded red Slug Bug to score a pound of heady cannabis and then watched "Magical Mystery Tour" while reclining on pillows in the long-gone and wonderfully groovy Dream Theater on Cannery Row.

    I took classes in ceramics at the local junior college, and one momentous and deliciously memorable afternoon I walked into the pottery lab and witnessed a sight of majesty and beauty that I had never imagined existed in this earthly life. I marveled dumbfounded at lanky and statuesque Paula bending over in her pink satin short *short* shorts as she mucked a lucky tray of clay for the upcoming pottery class. I managed somehow to invite that voluptuous classmate of mine to breakfast only to discover on her arrival, as she opened her plain mid-length brown cotton twill coat after finishing the French toast, that she was suddenly magnificently and awesomely naked and completely irresistible.

    That wonderful woman ushered me quickly into the carnal sanctuary of the proverbial older woman and initiated me in her special body of knowledge. Many times we stepped through "window panes" of lysergic acid diethylamide and cannabis into worlds of eroticism, passion, and fear. She taught me how to sew beautifully fabricked cowboy shirts with lace on the sleeves and collars with contrasting colors of satin piping. We lived together, gardened, cooked, hosted garden meals, and inevitably came down from the long high. I finally left because she wanted to settle (me) down, but I realized I had a lot of life to live before I could settle down. A beautiful spirit who would welcome me often in my solitary times of searching and loneliness—her beauty was simple, generous, and natural. She unlocked and opened forever in me a playground full of exquisitely stunning and alluring forces, full of danger and delight.

"It is extremely beautiful to belong to a woman, to give yourself. Don't laugh if I sound foolish. But to love a woman, you see, to abandon yourself to her, to absorb her completely and feel absorbed by her, that is not what you call 'being in love,' which you mock a little. For me it is the road to life, the way toward the meaning of life." xxxix

For a few years then, a few years before that late spring morning in 1986 when a nineteen-year old Mexican *señorita* who would become my wife and soul mate enrolled in my Advanced Intensive English class at the Salinas Adult School, I began to free fall into the exotic, erotic, melodic worlds of a few special Monterey Bay women — strong ones, the ones who are passionate to do or create something new, something wonderful, something never before—artists, creators, musicians, doers, fascinating women, the only kind I ever wanted to get close to.

Blond-haired, cherub-faced Greta wore long dark green and purple flowing or diaphanous white gauze gowns that did little to hide the alive peaks and glens of her alabaster skin. She chain-smoked unfiltered Marlboros, kissed like an angel on a limpid cloud, but tasted like a stale ashtray to the non-smoker. She spent her days behind an emerald four-panel door painting oval cream-colored eggs and more eggs on dark impasto canvases, large, bigger, and then huge canvases leaning against the high walls and that touched the crown molding of the creaky Victorian house where she and her husband and I lived.

She and I often drove along the scenic midnight vista of Highway One along Big Sur and parked on the high overlook of Hurricane Point where the silver reflections off the Pacific mirrored the silent passion we shared. Mercifully, one rapturous night she broke the emotional tension that had been accumulating layer by layer for months when she quietly defied her insecure and demanding husband by descending as if from the clouds of grey twilight onto the eager greenhorn to usher me into a blissful seventh heaven where I learned and practiced again and again the correct pronunciation of what was becoming my favorite word—ecstasy.

Greta left unexpectedly for New York one summer to hawk her giant eggs, and she never came back for more eggs or more of me. Who knows if her eggs ever hatched in The Big Apple? I moped around like an abandoned puppy all year waiting for her return. Only a romantic or an idiot would pine away all year for such a succulent kisser and honeyed lover. I finally realized that I had been dumped, a valuable lesson gifted early on in my life of relationships.

> "Only now it occurred to him that no words had been exchanged between Him and Lise, except at the very end, after the caresses were over, and then only a few and they had been insignificant. What long conversations he had had with Narcissus! But now, it seemed, he had entered a wordless world, in which one called to one another like owls, in which words had no meaning. He was ready for it. He had no more need for words today, or for thoughts; only for Lise, only for this wordless, blind, mute groping and searching, this sighing and melting." [xl]

Songbirds rarely cohabit with human beings, but Lark was an exquisite exception. Thick brunette hair, passionate in gesture and devotion, with flashing brown eyes that always led an insouciant toss of her head, gently expectant and waiting upon my wishes, at her ancient upright piano filling the emotional space between us with lilting melodies and a voice that soared like our lust never did. We wrote songs where my open string guitar tunings and her sweet melodic musings meandered across the fields of our affection. We penned lush calligraphic poems folded into hand-made mulberry paper envelopes full of sequins, old postage stamps, and special pressed flowers. We filled her ancient claw-foot bathtub with herb-scented hot water for each other's leisurely bath. Protracted walks and ardent kisses long into the foggy nights of Pacific Grove could not harmonize the subtle but persistent dissonance that played out *fortissimo* and *sotto voce* over several uncomfortable months. So hard to face the music as it diverged into two dissimilar keys, and our inamorato never did face things directly, unable to keep a songbird caged, so the beautiful reclusive swan winged off into the musical reflection of the Pacific Ocean. And there she remains.

> "All the time he was learning. In a short time he learned many kinds of love, many arts of love, absorbed the expediencies of many women. He also learned to see women in their multiplicity, how to feel, to touch, to smell them." [xli]
>
> "Quite soon he began to notice that the purpose of his wandering lay, perhaps, in this distinguishing, that he was perhaps driven from woman to woman in order to learn and exercise this gift of recognizing and differentiating still more subtly, more profoundly, with greater variation. Perhaps his destiny was to learn to know women and to learn love in a thousand ways, until he reached perfection…" [xlii]

Many times this young cadet left the old Thunderbird Restaurant in the Carmel Valley late night after his shift as waiter, and I would wrangle my decrepit faded navy blue '62 Falcon station wagon to the foot of a rickety Z of wooden stairs that squeaked up to a small tidy apartment where a petite and demure Katherine lived amid elegant white and ecru linen and lace, exquisite glassware and delicate china, and heavy mismatched silver place settings. Her thick nests of black hair, the milk chocolate smoothness of her skin, and the fawn-like expectancy of her lithe arms and legs suffused her tiny apartment with a soft and warm musky, wild aroma that drew me to her body as I tried remove the lid from the fragrant bubbling pan to smell and taste her secret-scented recipes. Teasing, taunting, feline, resisting, and so delicious, the meals she served only me became a game of cat and mouse, chase and conquer, and if she ever did return to her oafish lineman husband, I was certain she never described to the hapless cornuto the boundaries of decency we transgressed during our brief but memorable preoccupation.

> "Experience taught him that every woman was beautiful and able to bring joy, that a mousy creature whom men ignored was capable of extraordinary fire and devotion, that the wilted had more maternal, mourning sweet tenderness, that

each woman had her secrets and her charms, and to unlock these made him happy. In that respect, all women were alike. Lack of youth or beauty was always balanced by some special gesture." [xliii]

"Love and ecstasy were to him the only truly warming things that gave life its value." [xliv]

"Women, the game of the sexes, came first in his list, and his frequent accesses of melancholy and disgust grew out of the knowledge that desire was a transitory, fleeting experience." [xlv]

Odd, wondrous rather, how, in hindsight, a lusty and warmhearted seamstress, a heavenly painter, an elusive songbird, and an Abyssinian temptress could all coalesce into one of the many dimensionless yet persistent narrative streams in a man's erotic consciousness. Such revered streams flow on for as long as I breathe out into the sea of what inevitably is becoming an old man's life, and the widening currents are certain to return with me without a whisper into the undifferentiated ocean of the divine, transcendent Atman, beyond the world of eroticism, change, and death. For now the differentiation between man and woman, the creative and the receptive, drives me more deeply inside my own manhood to seek the female, the balance of which the external world is but a shimmering reflection.

"All existence seemed to be based on duality, on contrast. Either one was a man or one was a woman, whether a wanderer or a sedentary burgher, either a thinking person or a feeling person—no one could breathe in at the same time as he breathed out, be a man as well as a woman, experience freedom as well as order, combine instinct and mind. One always had to pay for the one with the loss of the other, and one thing was always just as important and desirable as the other. Perhaps women had it easier in this respect. Nature had created them in such a way that desire bore its fruit automatically, that the bliss of love became a child. For a man, eternal longing replaced this simple fertility. Was the god who had created everything in this manner an evil god, was he hostile, did he laugh ironically at his own creation? No, he could not be evil; he had created the hart and the roebuck, fish and birds, forests, flowers, the seasons. But the split ran through his entire creation. Perhaps it had not turned out right or was incomplete—or did God intend this lack, this longing in human life for a special purpose? Was this perhaps the seed of the enemy, or original sin? But why should this longing and this lack be sinful? Did not all that was beautiful and holy, all that man created and gave back to God as a sacrifice of thanks spring from this very lack, from this longing?" [xlvi]

As I stepped ever so gently across one woman's doorstep to another, I never stopped thinking about the apparent dichotomy between passion and spirituality, how monks take vows of celibacy to focus their energy into their spiritual development without the distractions of women and children to sidetrack their development, and how contradictory sexuality and the monastic life seemed on the surface. I recalled again and again and thought repeatedly about what Hermann Hesse had portrayed and described so eloquently, and what my dear friend, Brother Paul, had written so frequently in his letters, about bringing prayer and sex together into a closer relationship.

In so many of his letters he wrote about the *intellectual* conflict between his passionate and sexual expression of love for the different people he loved in and out of the monastery and his commitment to the monastic community and lifestyle. He never was able to love anyone in any kind of formally sanctioned relationship like boyfriend-girlfriend or marriage, and he always struggled with his commitment and vows as a monk and the undeniable force of his passion to connect with the men and women he loved in his life. His relief and solace in telling me about his sexuality and the people he had and still loved, how he treasured my acceptance of him the way he was, how he valued my love for him, how he recognized the passion we both shared as men who loved others...that was one of our greatest blessings, and I know how relieved he was for me to know..

> *They were relationships of real love, expressed very sexually and (as I would feel today) very prayerfully. They seem similar to your remarks about your own sexual life. They make me wonder if it might not help everybody to bring prayer and sex into closer relationship. Would your book possibly be a good place to do that?* [xlvii]

So much of the monastic life is orchestrated by rituals, schedules, observances, ways of behavior that you are supposed to follow, like getting in step with everyone else for a mutually agreed upon purpose. But I came to understand that that is not what passion is. Passion is like the sudden laughter that changes everything for a precious timeless moment, the unexpected touch or embrace of love or reconciliation, the startling wave of lust that overcomes the moment and pulls you into the realm of another person. It's a wordless door into someone's sanctuary where the locks and keys to the puzzle of all their little mysteries are safeguarded yet faintly revealed. It's the hunger that sweeps away words and ideas and preconceptions with the electric splendor of smooth cool skin, with the sweet and pungent smells of living bodies' excitement and presentation, with profuse bouquets of piquant taste buds and secret flavors.

> *In your cover letter you said that you "think the relatively intimate specifics of our different personalities is what makes the story so compelling." I agree, but I'm really ambiguous about the possibility of my sex life being published. Ironically I touched on the problem in my letter of 13 June 93, on page 78: "...my sexuality became something I never discussed with anybody. I locked it up inside me, tighter than a drum, threw away the key and joined religious life, where there was no sex. Or so I thought..."* [xlviii]

No monk, I had finally come to understand, could ever say truthfully that his experience of losing himself in God was any better, more profound or meaningful, or somehow more eternal than the letting go of all thought, presence, perception and identity in that eternal momentary release and uncontrollable radiation of burning light and silver liquid that can unite and mingle one mortal human being so intimately with another.

> *...there's a real fascination with the idea of getting the story out, dropping the mask, being free at last... I wasn't expecting it, but I'm really glad you did. It makes me face some real challenges, and that's good for the spirit... So your ol' buddy, while trying to be a good celibate monk and devote his whole life to God, still falls in love with all kinds of God's people... Is this my thorn in the flesh, which, like Paul, I should pray to be rid of? Or do I pray that I learn to live with it, even to delight in it...?* [xlix]

Perhaps that's the only thing different about the monastic life, I often mused, that monks pull themselves apart from normal life trying to live on the deepest levels of being, thinking that life in the world somehow obscures the heart of the deepness, assuming that life presents us with experiences that detract us from reality, as if only in the monastery one could uncover the underlying essence that is supposedly unavailable to people outside the monastery.

That is why I left the monastery. I knew that reality, that the essence, was everywhere, not just in New Clairvaux Abbey. I didn't have to limit or restrict myself to find it. I only had to look wherever I was, and I would find it, right there, where it had always been, always is, everywhere...just under the surface of the day-to-day humdrum, lurking, waiting beneath an ever-so thin transparent mental veil, intact, sacrosanct perhaps, but there all the same, available, ready, there...no, here...the monastery in your heart. As Master Thomas Merton wrote:

> "There is in all visible things an invisible fecundity, a dimmed light, a meek namelessness, a hidden wholeness. This mysterious Unity and Integrity is Wisdom, the Mother of all, *Natura Naturans*. There is in all things an inexhaustible sweetness and purity, a silence that is a fountain of action and

of joy. It rises up in wordless gentleness and flows out to me from the unseen roots of all created being..." [1]

Marriage One

Whoever first scratched the phrase, "The Seven Year Itch," into the archives of matrimonial breakdown most probably never heard of the Feigenbaum constant ($\delta = 4.6692...$), the number that predicts when and how many natural phenomena develop, split, and branch off into two predictable directions. It's not so improbable then that I would eventually be mired in the legal repeating decimal of liquidating financial assets in the community property state of bliss, California. Seven years before that, on the last day that a twenty-dollar marriage license was valid, the only justice of the peace my first wife and I could locate by phone in Monterey pronounced us husband and wife inside his lime green upholstered front room overlooking Old Monterey and the Bay itself, and I became the lawful wedded husband of one of the best draftswomen and fabric artists I have ever known.

We rented an uninsulated two-bedroom Victorian in Salinas, and settled down stacking all shelving surfaces with art materials, some mine, mostly hers. Bolts and folded mounds of fabrics of every texture and color; raw fibers like sisal, raffia, rope, cotton and linen strings; found wooden and mineral objects including bamboo, horsetail, and twigs of all distortion; stacks of rice and mulberry papers with all sizes of sumi-e brushes and inks; hard and soft pencils and charcoals, colored pencils, crayons, glues, and tubes of acrylic paints; arts and crafts tools like staplers, scissors, knives, Japanese draw saws, several sewing machines, paper cutters, aluminum straightedges, French curves, compasses, and tackle boxes full of hidden found and art treasure. She and I constructed there a nest of pure, raw, creative beauty from which anything we imagined we could and did create.

We borrowed fifty-grand from my big-hearted father, bought 7 acres in the rolling hills outside of town in Prunedale, and designed and owner-built on a hill facing south the first passive solar house in Monterey County. It had an attached greenhouse, exposed concrete thermal mass, large Douglas fir beams, a wood stove as the only back-up heat source, double glazing, two by six walls, and a full shop in the garage, the simplest of passive styles. We conceived first a girl there, then a boy, all the while not knowing that *she* was doing this for *me* while quietly thinking that in exchange *I* was doing that for *her*, an unspoken relationship of deal-making, the undoing of a marital knot whose ends unraveled completely one night after a year of futile marital counseling.

God bless Irwin, master therapist from Sunrise House, who, after a year of smiling back and forth at us while we idled in neutral one momentous evening, looked me straight in the eye as I sat next to my voiceless wife and said in a shockingly casual tone of voice, "Mr. Frode, if you want something to change, *you* will have to do something about it." Five minutes into the stone-cold drive back to our now cold solar house, I uttered the words that would squeeze all happiness out of the following few years like a pair of emotional vice-grip pliers.

"I'm going to file for divorce."

I never knew if the distant neighbors called 911 that night as my soon-to-dematerialize wife suddenly scuttled up the hillside by our house and began an ancient keening, wailing, and screaming hours into the unheeding night as if she was being flayed alive or disemboweled. I listened to her unrelenting tortuous screams, and my own entrails contracted uncontrollably as I groked the implications of the decision *I* had finally, finally made.

> "But mind and will lived within him nevertheless; he was an artist, and this made his life rich and difficult. Any life expands and flowers only through division and contradiction. What are reason and sobriety without the knowledge of intoxication? What is sensuality without death standing behind it? What is love without the eternal mortal enmity of the sexes?" [li]

My decision to divorce the talented and strong woman with whom I had lived and raised two wonderful children oozed with doubt, pain, and guilt. I would always bear willingly the responsibility for the sundering of a marriage, the price to pay for wrenching free from inertia, complacency, and dissatisfaction. Years earlier I had left the monastery in a similar way—wailing, with the gnashing of teeth, mine, far from the ones I loved, with no one to embrace, alone with my own verdict and my own punishment. Then, I would be leaving the first man I ever loved. In this case, I would be leaving the best artist I had every known and the woman I never loved.

The very day she disappeared without a word from the house we had built, and took the children with her, leaving only her lawyer's business card; I was shaking hands with Doctor David in the office of the Salinas Adult School, where I had been teaching English as a Second Language full time for several years, meeting the only other man beside Brother Paul I ever loved. *Everyone* loved David, everyone except his wife who had nudged him up north from LA to start afresh—no wife, new life, new business location. He was a big teddy bear with a barrel chest, and it was clear that his arms were muscular from adjusting people's spines and necks again and again for years. All his patients came back for more, more of good ol' Doctor David. He would put your head in a chiropractic half-nelson, distract you by blowing in your ear, then when you were wondering why in the hell he just blew in your ear, even though you knew why and what was coming, he would suddenly crank your neck around for all you were worth until all the vertebra snapped into place like firecrackers on the 4th.

David was a healer in every sense of the word, one of the two men in my life who was and still is my dearest friend, my spiritual mentor, and my colleague in living life to the fullest and deepest. On his wanderings Goldmund had eventually found the artist and sculpture, Master Niklaus, who helped Goldmund find and manifest his own beloved mother long dead through sculpture and art.

> "He knew only this: that he greatly admired Master Niklaus, but in no way loved him as he had Narcissus...This, it seemed, was linked to the contrasts in the master's nature..."
> lii

And so indulge me now as I indulge myself to slow down on a short detour along the frontage road of a different friendship that mattered deeply between two odd creative men who recognized each other from the first strong handshake and embrace. It was David who became my Master Nicklaus, and it was he who showed me a way of being human that I would carry with me as I did the passion I shared with Brother Paul.

Doctor David

When I disassembled my first marriage, my dear mother, June, bought me a new Toyota Celica GT to take my mind off meeting with and changing divorce attorneys, not seeing my kids for weeks, and paying exorbitant legal fees. Perfectly timed, my best buddy, Doctor David, and I took off on a two week jaunt to Arizona ostensibly to visit his ex-girlfriend. After all, he too had just separated from his screaming wife.

We slept in tiny cramped trailer-hotels in the Navajo nation, ate the longest and hottest chile rellenos in a huge restaurant at the Navaho crossroads of Tuba City, salivated over the enormity of the Grand Canyon, felt the spirits of many native people long gone but present in the hidden caves we climbed up to in Bandelier Park, were silenced by the grandeur and beauty of Canyon de Chelly, froze our asses off in his girlfriend's hot tub while it was snowing and bone cold, stayed in little rundown snowed-in inns in the Sierra Nevada mountains, got my first speeding ticket in Nevada for going ninety, and took more pictures of David and me than I ever had reason to.

This was our quest without women, and with David and I, it was a spiritual quest. Although he and I never spoke of The Spirit or God, I recognize now that he was also a seeker of the Ultimate, and ultimately a master in his own right. I wouldn't be surprised if David's spirit returned to one of those caves high up in the south-facing cliffs in Bandelier Park where we huddled wordless one winter day and looked out over our futures.

Every weekend for almost a year while we were separated and estranged from wives and from our four children, David and I monopolized each other's lives. Sometimes he would show up unannounced in one of his classic restored Mercedes 300Ds, and we would take off to LA aircraft surplus stores and come back with all colors of wire ties; small threaded aluminum fittings; tiny brass or black anodized aluminum wood and machine screws with matching washers and nuts; assortments of Plexiglas and Lexan rods, tubes, sheets, and blocks; scraps of brass wire mesh, diamond plate, aluminum and brass plate, and corrugated metal sheeting; the tiniest of drill bits; all manner of jewelry fittings in silver and gold; all shapes of tiny metal files; cotton buffing wheels, sticks of white and red rouge, emery, and Tripoli for polishing and buffing; and scraps of polyethylene, polypropylene, polycarbonate, PVC, heat-shrink plastics, Teflon sheet, and Styrofoam.

    We spent months of days and nights in the sanctuary of my basement shop creating jewelry from our gatherings that we married with pearls, diamonds, tourmalines, and crystals. Our collaboration over those few months catalyzed and released startling latent female energies that our ex-wives had obstructed unknowingly, but the jewelry (we named "Trendecco") was so avant-garde and out there that even Meyer Brier Weiss in San Francisco and the original Running Ridge Gallery in Ojai thought their "clientele wasn't sophisticated enough" for our work. That was that. The making was the joy for David and me. In my garage there still lurks a large, mysterious, time capsule-like cardboard box full of the objects we pulled up and out from the depths of our shared vision of how the three dimensions of beauty could scintillate, glow, and astonish.

> "In art, in being an artist, Goldmund saw the possibility of reconciling his deepest contradictions, or at least expressing newly and magnificently the split in his nature..." [liii]

    On other memorable occasions David would call on Thursday nights and ask for my "Yes" or "No" for backpacking, then show up at six on Friday night in his cherry International Harvester Travel All with its original sea foam green paint and roof rack. I would have all ready to throw into the truck what we always took—spinning and fly fishing equipment; a small arsenal containing 9 mm pistols, .38 Specials, high caliber rifles and assorted shotguns, plus ammo (David loved hollow points) for each weapon; backpacks, tents, axes, saws, a good assortment of wire ties, and rope; wine, beer, sake, and food enough for in-camp or on-the-trail gourmet cooking. Many trips I relish recalling now epitomized our high adventures.

Winding step-by-step up a steep trail known only to Doctor David high up into California's Los Padres Mountains we carried only backpacks, food, cooking gear, sleeping bags, rain wear, and shotguns with stuffed magazines. That summer evening we arrived in an isolated high mountain meadow covered completely with blue and occasional genetically mutated white lupines, and we made camp by a fire ring used for years by Basque sheepherders. We shot, cooked over oak wood, and ate several fat quail, boiled long grain brown rice till that crisp brown crust formed on the bottom, and then savored several aluminum camp cups of hot sake under a full moon next to the roaring fire pyromaniac David always kept at the edge of anarchy. Rising the next morning to stir and reinvigorate the embers, we boiled handfuls of coffee grounds, then steeped dried apricots and oatmeal, and while we waited for breakfast to materialize, we savored the cold dawn silence of the high, uninhabited mountains without the need to speak, ask, or answer. On the hike back out I literally stumbled on a rusted bell used around the neck of a mule, the kind of bell that sounded from one valley to the next. I am holding it now as I remember the crystalline clear voice it had then. David was one of the few men I've known who was truly intimate and at home with silence.

Another frame from the 35-millimeter film of our relationship shows us hiking up a steep hillside in the Los Padres congested and overgrown with madrone, live oak, and pine. With backpacks, raingear, and carrying our ever-present 12 gauge pumps, we confronted an evening storm that suddenly inundated the entire valley up onto the mountainside where we stood watching the arrival of the storm. David and I began yelling suddenly like madmen, shouting into the torrential rain and wind while we loosed Remington magnum #4 buckshot up into the looming black clouds as the gale taunted and laughed back at us unafraid. Guns for David and for me were not instruments of random violence or destruction but precision tools of passion and beauty. I still have the first gun I owned—a Taurus .38 Special he picked up for me at one of those ubiquitous gun shows at the Boise Fair Grounds.

Frame number three shows us following a winding dirt road that spiraled down into a Sierra Nevada valley near Oakhurst, his California place of birth, an area neither of us had ever been in, spiraling down and down on dirt and gravel in my new celebrating-my-divorce-present-from-my-dear-mother Toyota Celica GT, and arriving at the actual unbelievable end of the dirt road in the middle of a Douglas Fir forest. We spent a frantic hour at David's urging searching around the area and piling up downed wood in what served as a clearing. Then David fed his greedy and scary mania for fire by creating a conflagration that threatened to ignite the tops of the trees so that *even he* grimaced and wondered about the sagacity of giving in to his compulsion. We stayed awake entranced with fire until we could safely fall asleep in the front seat of my car.

Frame four is David and I wading deep back into the shadowed headwaters of a gurgling mountain stream in Big Sur, steadying ourselves around the huge boulders, stopping here and there to feel the spirits of the water and trees, peering through the clear water to see the mottled greens and browns of the stream bed. As the forest closed in around and over us and the stream, we each found our separate boulders where we sat, let go of thought and individual identity, and we merged for hours with The Self that inhabited the natural setting there and that flowed into the Pacific Ocean by beautiful Lime Kiln Creek where we had taken our boys to camp by water and just be guys.

The fifth frame is located on the very top of a mountain whose name I cannot recall where we had driven all afternoon then made a tent-less camp around his International hoping to enjoy the silence and view uninterrupted by humans. An unexpected band of several motorcyclists arrived after midnight, set up camp three-hundred feet from us, and began shooting off beer rockets by setting can after can of Coors in a trough formed from two long 2 x 4's nailed together the end of which scorched and flamed in the fire so that when the beer boiled, the pop-tops burst, and the beer rockets shot off into the night with a whoooosh that sounded like banshees.

David and I walked over casually to welcome them to the mountaintop with our shotguns chambered and cradled in our arms and our .38 Smith and Wessons holstered around our waists. We introduced ourselves, handed them a six-pack of Coors, and mentioned what an awesome coincidence it was that we all had come all the way to the top of the mountain to find such a tranquil and quiet scene.

    David and I looked for every opportunity to cut open sacks and sacks of sand, Portland cement, and gravel, and we hoed yards and yards of concrete in my contractor's wheelbarrow to form steps, planters, walkways, walls, anything we could imagine in reverse, formed up with plywood, 2 x 4s, our beloved sheetrock screws, and then reveal in all its imperfect splendor as we stripped off the creaking forms. We climbed up into giant overgrown valley oaks on my Prunedale property, and David showed me how to feel the spirit of a tree to know what branches and limbs needed to be pruned, and we pruned high, *very high*, in the trees with saws and loppers all afternoon. We felled with double-headed axes two tall eucalyptus trees that were ten feet apart, and in the spirit of competition the one who felled his tree first had to use his chain saw to cut up his tree first; then, we could roll the chunks of aromatic fresh wood downhill where we took a week splitting up the green wood with sledgehammers, wedges, muscle, and sweat. One morning David and I went bonkers with his great idea to cut a road up the hillside of my property, and while burning brush with a backpack pump sprayer filled with diesel, he finally ignited enough full grown eucalyptus trees to motivate me to run down to the house and call the local fire department to put out the fire. I had never known a true spiritual pyromaniac until David.

    On the road a lot to buy materials to make things, David and I ambled through all kinds of checkout lines. I watched how he joked simply with every checker as if they were old friends, and I noted how each one's working face lit up with a spark of human happiness for just that one brief moment. I started to imitate his easy and natural manner with people and have been ever grateful for such a lesson. I cooked day-long feasts with David—Thanksgiving, Christmas, Easter, and ordinary Sundays, and from our humble kitchens came roasts of pig, lamb, or beef, glazed with his homemade cherry or plum chutneys; turkeys stuffed with his homemade cornbread, chestnuts, his mother's sausage, and leeks; quiches with carrots erupting from the bubbly brown surface like missiles ready for takeoff; leavened and unleavened breads full of his favorite flax, sunflower, sesame, oats, and walnuts; cooked millet, brown rices, quinoa, and lentils spiced with coconut, chiles, cinnamon, paprikas, coriander, cumin, pepper, and raisins; and huge popovers pulled from the oven still blisteringly hot, loaded with nut butters and honey and dripping down cheeks, chins, and onto shirtfronts. Feasts they were, and the flavors' many dimensions remain in my mind and heart.

When David started to experience a strange weakness in his body, he thought it was from the mercury in the fillings in his teeth, and we all chuckled behind his back when he had all the supposedly guilty fillings removed. It wasn't until it was obvious that he had Lou Gehrig's disease that he finally quietly handed off his chiropractic practice to a colleague and readied himself for the inevitable. It is one of life's damned ironies, damned, that I was in the process of moving my entire family to Idaho when David was flat on his back at home on oxygen writing a few end-of-life terse and comical phrases on a dry-erase board his son, Thuri, would hold for him.

I brought him a small water-washed stone, wire-tied to a section of bamboo that we had made a few years before at Lime Kiln Creek, one of our characteristically wonderful spontaneous *shibui* creations he and I relished making. I told him that I loved him, and I departed reluctantly for the North. A month later on my way out of town I wheeled into the Prunedale grange hall, parked the largest Penske truck available full of my giant timber bamboo plants (our favorites), then stood quietly at the back of the room where hundreds and hundreds of his friends were remembering him and celebrating his life with pictures and stories. I hugged his two sons and his ex, and I left feeling full that I knew him and hollow that he was gone. So quickly gone.

I learned from my dear friend David two simple secrets of being a human being:

- Conduct yourself with each person as if she or he is your beloved brother or sister. In doing so, there are no preconceived or vestigial walls between you preventing the easy and natural exchange of acknowledgement and appreciation as fellow human beings.
- David also showed me through our countless doings and makings the two behavioral polarities that make action and art so powerful. First, eliminate the mental chasm of doubt and uncertainty between a good idea and acting on that idea. Second, freely drop whatever you are doing to do something more worthwhile.

These two dynamic polarities of how reality is manifested from ideas are the core of freedom and creativity. I thank David daily for such a blessing that has allowed me to live and act with both authority and humility. I cannot imagine a greater gift or legacy. David was a natural teacher and a student of life.

Brother Paul opened wide the doors of love for me as did Narcissus for Goldmund; Doctor David taught me to be an artist as Master Niklaus did for Goldmund. Both men showed me the two polarities of being a human being, the two worlds of mind and of feeling. David had no fear, just *joie de vivre*, and everything he ever was he shared with those who were close with him. He was generous, loving, conflicted, and beautifully human, a man's man, a woman's man. I wish David could have met Brother Paul. What a meeting of men *that* would have been.

I still wait silently for them here in Idaho, an expatriate from my world of men. Their spirits could have soared here.

I call upon them each morning to be with me. They are.

Chapter 10: Soul Mate

"All my longings, all my dreams and sweet anguish, all the secrets that slept within me, came awake, everything was transformed and enchanted, everything made sense. She taught me what a woman is and what secrets she had. In half an hour she aged me by many years. I know many things now." [liv]
Hermann Hesse
Narcissus and Goldmund

Do you remember how in Hesse's novel, <u>Narcissus and Goldmund</u> started out together in the abbey? Then Goldmund left, and Narcissus remained. Toward the end of the book and the end of their lives, Narcissus wondered if life had passed him by. As my own life on earth draws to its close, I sometimes wonder the same. What would it have been like to have lived the primordial life of marrying and begetting that you have lived? [lv]
Brother Paul Williams

    AND THEN I MET ELVIRA.

Sashaying into my classroom she dumbfounded me with the dark and smoldering flame of her presence. Invisible around her, it was as if cold mountain streams were gurgling up from hidden and shadowed glens. Unseen but remembered ferns, bromeliads, and jungle orchids glistened in her warm high mountain mists. Small furred mammals scurrying to their dens across her rain forest floor chittered and yelped from an unseen dimension. Far-away and mysterious sylvan grottos beckoned where high waterfalls splash forever into deep blue pools where she waited. I have never forgotten the moment. Across a classroom full of Mexican, Columbian, Chilean, Thai, Vietnamese, and Middle Eastern English language learners, all chatting, gossiping, and snacking—I felt the euphony of her aura, and a sudden shiver raced up my back and nested in my brain.

She swept into the room accompanied by a few of her friends, already my students, and they sauntered over to my desk to introduce the new student to the maestro. I understood even before she told me her name was Elvira that what people commonly lampooned as love at first sight was a real event, a 3-dimensional revelation of mystery, the deep harmonic of spiritual and emotional attraction embodied only occasionally in two human beings. I know now what I had no way of comprehending then, that The Great Spirit was about to entrust me with a gift that only I would be able to safeguard, nurture, and sooner than I ever expected, to husband. To this day I still am not sure if she was, and still is in truth, a nymph or a naiad, some kind of creature born of water, mountains, or trees, come from some preverbal natural world; where boundaries between aware beings are permeable and indistinct—where perception is an act of love; where sentience assumes myriad forms of melody and rhythm—both harmonious and dissonant; and where awareness is guided by aroma and fragrance—pheromones, flowers, and herbs alike.

> "Even there one had to be lucky, find a special friendship, a readiness. It was fortunate that love did not need words; or else it would be full of misunderstanding and foolishness." [lvi]

I shook her delicate hand and savored the warmth in her slender fingers as I introduced myself, asked her in English where she was from, and looked into her wide brown eyes as she told me confidently that she had been sent from Beginning to Advanced English because she knew too much to stay in beginning classes.

"I mean, what country are you from?" I heard myself ask as I held her right hand politely in mine. I felt my heart and mind being lifted up out of the ongoing chaos, anger, confusion, and alienation of an ugly and protracted divorce by the presence of this petite, elfin young woman in front of me. I listened to her words often mispronounced yet always expressive while I let invisible currents of warmth and attraction flow between us with a sudden sense of gratitude and relief, a sensation that I had never or ever since felt.

> "How strange it was with women and loving! There really was no need for words…everything else had been said without words. Then how had she said it? With her eyes, yes, and with a certain intonation in her slightly thick voice, and with something more, a scent perhaps, a subtle discreet emanation of the skin, by which women and men were able to know at once when they desired one another. It was strange, like a subtle, secret language." [lvii]

While she was telling me that she was from Yuriria, a little town close to the capital of Morelia in the state of Guanajuato, Mexico, that she lived an hour south of Salinas in King City, and that she was coming into the Adult School every day to learn English; I was at the same time noticing the guarded and discreet way she glanced away and then back at me. With my eyes I tried inconspicuously to trace the sensuous contours of her full scarlet-colored lips and prominent thinly contoured ears, the short tomboyish cut of her ebony-colored hair, and her confident yet impish demeanor and stance just a foot away from me. I didn't know that I was looking at the rest of my life.

Although she was that close, she was as far away and inaccessible to me as the court system is aloof and detached from the day-to-day exigencies of mortal beings. It would be a year before she would step out of my classroom, and I would step boldly into her world where we would both be free to let unseen forces of culture, family, harmony, and love begin to manifest themselves in us.

"Welcome to the class, Elvira. We start in ten minutes."

She thanked me, turned around gaily arm-in-arm with Griselda, Miguel, and Lupe, and sauntered out into the hallway. I knew, even though she didn't look back at me, that in both our separate brains, old, old, very old neural circuits long ago forgotten were lighting up with electric excitement, and new neuronal pathways of hope and renewal were being opened up moment-by-moment, thought-by-thought, as I let myself wonder over and over what it would be like to wander and delight in that young gamine's world.

After that day when she swept into my classroom, I began to wait, not knowing exactly why or for what, only that there was something about that young woman that marshaled my will and intentions in her emotional and physical direction. We chatted at breaks, she was one of the quickest and most astute learners I had ever taught, and when she left a hand-written note of appreciation and respect on my desk, I understood the unseen dimension of her gesture. I responded to her probe with my own note of thanks and appreciation, appropriately modulated to mirror the intensity and depth of hers. I would anticipate the next *billet-doux*, sometimes positioned discreetly on my desk, left casually in my mailroom slot, or eventually tucked securely under a windshield wiper of my car in the parking lot across the street. I learned of her guileless proclivity—green apples, and we soon were waiting for the lunch break when we would share tart apples and sweet conversation. By the time I was bringing her miniature calla lilies wrapped in the previous day's newspaper, she had graduated from my Advanced Intensive English class, and was enrolled in Early Childhood Education classes at the local community college.

We were free from the propriety and protocol that had kept us cautious, restrained, and not unexpectedly, eager for more apples. We discovered out-of-town and out-of-the-way, l950s El Rancho Motel on the recommendation of a player colleague of mine, and there were more days than usual those glorious months when I suddenly felt ill and had to arrange a substitute for my classes. I would wait anxiously for the onset of a cold, the flu, or a cough every few weeks, and when I felt bad enough, I would pick up the phone and make two phone calls, one for a substitute for my class and one to make a room reservation. Calla lilies, two bottles of Freixenet in a red and white plastic cooler, a cardboard box lid packed with bulging little white cartons of Chinese food, "I Love Lucy" reruns on the motel TV, and a bilingual edition of Pablo Neruda formed the external ornamentation of our celebration. It was those days of leisure, passion, levity, laughing, and sleep that we now recall often with a fond laugh, a hug, and a kiss knowing that now, when there are early departures for the salt mines, we can sometimes relapse easily to that sensuous, sybaritic S curve of togetherness we still always find healing—home-cooked love-food for our spirits and hearts.

> "Ah, how Lise's half-closed eyes had looked almost blind at the height of ecstasy; only the white had shown through the slits of twitching lids—ten thousand learned or lyrical words could not express it! Nothing, ah, nothing at all could be expressed—and yet, again and again one felt the urge to speak, the urge to think." lviii

We were obligated to idle a year before we could fly to Yuriria, Mexico, where I would marry that lovely *señorita* in the 16th century cathedral of Saint Augustine in a ceremony completely in Spanish. When I followed her against her adamant wishes to her mother and father's little whitewashed bungalow by a hollyhock-covered hillock in King City, we found her parents in the tiny front room waiting patiently for us as if they had received what could only be a psychic message that we were on our way. The two interrogators and the witness sat down stoically on the tired sofa, and I, the defendant, fidgeting in the hard-backed cross-examination chair sat alone facing them with only three feet of space between us. After a few moments I quickly interpreted the uncomfortable silence to mean that I should speak. It was up to me.

Oh, my God! It suddenly struck me, *they only speak Spanish!*

"*Buenas tardes, Señor Gomez*," I swallowed hard and began slowly in the best college Spanish I could muster, "*Estamos aqui porque yo quiero casarme con su hija, Elvira.*"

It was the most important sentence in Spanish I have ever spoken in my life except for the *"Si, Accepto"* I mumbled into the microphone the Mexican priest thrust toward my face after he asked me *en español* if I would take this Elvira for my lawful wedded wife. When I thought I had agreed with Señor Gomez that, of course, we could be wed the following summer in their Mexican home town, two faces slowly thawed to smiles, but Elvira frowned furtively at me because all along she had wanted to just forget the whole damn thing, it was that stressful for her. In spite of *her* chagrin, Elvira's parents produced a large bottle of red wine on the small wooden table along with a pan of spicy steak with *chile negro* sauce and handmade tortillas. We ate together in the small room lit by a bare 40 watt bulb in its white porcelain ceiling fixture, and although it was an uncomfortable and uneasy public display of commitment and acceptance of the divorced gringo with two children from a previous marriage, both Elvira and I have now come to understand that the asking of her hand in marriage and the simple dinner afterwards set in motion harmonious forces of learning, understanding, and healing that would reverberate for many many years across borders of language, custom, and country. And so it has been. Wonderful worlds have been created with our families' cultural intermingling.

Nevertheless, we would be glancing at each other with eyebrows raised when weeks later Elvira's mother and father plunked themselves down in the two seats immediately behind us on the Aero Mexico flight to Mexico where we would be married. She whispered to me that they were chaperoning us, making sure we didn't kiss or worse on the plane before we each affirmed, "*Accepto*," the following week in the historical cathedral of Saint Augustine in her home town. We dared not even utter to each other the words "El Rancho Motel" or act like we had been more physically familiar with each other than shaking hands. We actually had already married in a courthouse civil ceremony in her hometown two days before flying to Mexico to be *really* married in a Catholic Church ceremony.

We had rented a small hall at the hot and dusty King City fairgrounds for the reception party afterwards, and I brought boxes of plates, silverware, and glasses from A-1 Rents. Doctor David brought dozens of huge dahlias of every color and shape from his own lush garden. My other two long-time best friends, Kurt and Kap, showed up as best men, and my two children, Piper and Miles, were there as flower-children. My dear mother, June, and brother, John, had driven from Salinas for the event. Elvira's best friend's mother made turkey with mole and rice and home-made tortillas, and we poured twelve bottles of Cazadores tequila and six bottles of Freixenet brut until there was no more. Her friends from Hartnell

College classes congratulated her and fantasized about their future husbands. At eight sharp we packed up the rental plates, silverware, and glassware for me to return to A-l Rents, and I drove alone back home to Salinas while my wife returned to her home still with her parents in King City. Not the first time, nor the last that I would wait for her. We laugh at it now.

Within two days we arrived in Mexico City where my wife's brother, academic genius and headmaster of the Autonomous University of Chapingo in Texcoco—the ancient capital of the Aztecs— put us up for the night in his small home at the agricultural training university. Elvira later told me that her father and mother were scandalized that his overfed, finicky, reputedly nymphomaniac wife served us large bowls of menudo for dinner—traditional soup made from pig's feet and intestines, believed incorrectly by Mexicans to be abhorrent to non-Mexicans—to see what the young divorced gringo was made of. Their skepticism faded after I asked for another bowl of the steaming hot and spicy broth.

Later in Yuriria, I was housed in another brother's house, the local surgeon and clinic owner, a house two blocks from Elvira's family house, far enough in their thinking to prevent any premarital improprieties, so important in Mexico where culture and religion are intertwined and often mistaken for each other. Every morning I was served pancakes, toast, Wheaties or Cheerios, milk, coffee, juice, and cut fruit to ensure that the gringo boy would have his gringo breakfast.

One of Elvira's other eight brothers, a perfectionist agronomist engineer—who turned out to be a macho Mexican Henry Higgins when he married and tried disastrously to save and perfect his own Eliza Doolittle from the local vegetable stand—had refused to greet his sister or me upon our arrival at the Mexico City airport because his sister was going to marry a divorced white man with two children, anathema in the socially correct Gomez family. Ironically, within a day I was accompanying him on pick up trips around the county, bouncing down dirt roads rounding up supplies for the wedding reception—live pigs for carnitas; boxes of rum and apple cider; beer, beer, and more beer; arrangements with several women to make the hundreds of tortillas by hand; the triple-layer wedding *tres leches* cake; two mariachi groups and two *conjuntos* to provide for a memorable battle of the four bands during the reception; hundreds of chairs to be unstacked and restacked; tables and tablecloths; and scores of waiters. His generosity has always been easy and heart-felt, always oriented inwards towards family cohesiveness and well-being. To this day I get along more easily with him than with most other of her siblings.

I had never in my life seen so many female cousins, nieces, sisters, aunts, and sisters-in-law gather in one place to make tissue and crepe paper flowers for the close to a dozen cars chosen for the wedding procession from the family home downhill to the church, then from the church to the reception. Long, wide, and low-slung whale-like Thunderbirds, Buicks, Pontiacs, and the ubiquitous Ford pickups were taped up with so many pink, white, and red flowers that it was difficult to determine the actual color of the fading paint on each car. It is a well-known fact that my wife was (and continues to be, in my relatively objective opinion) the family *consentida*, the overindulged one, being the last born of eleven, and because she had returned from El Norte with a relatively well-off gringo on her hooks, she was adored by the many family girls as royalty, a family princess.

Only a princess would have all her childhood clothes custom-made by the town seamstress. Only she would pout and shake her head until her hapless and helpless father surrendered to the most elegant and expensive Petite Jean high heels for her to sport in the local tractor parades. Only my Elvira could expect that her wedding dress be custom-made at the only fashion boutique in the state where wives of politicians from Guanajuato's capital, Morelia, are chauffeured to have the newest couture designs from New York let out and sent to their gated Colonial houses. When I finally beheld her dress on our wedding day, I was stunned to think how much time and effort it took the seamstresses to sew so many pearls on one dress. To this day we refer appropriately to her matching silver-white high heels as the Cinderella Shoes.

Everyone was overjoyed and stressed to the limit of excitement when the grimacing bride (having more of those vexing second thoughts about getting married) finally took her place in the newest and largest flower-festooned vehicle to lead the procession the five blocks to the church. Now, it rarely rains in Guanajuato in spite of the fact that it is called the Bread Basket of Mexico; so, when, two minutes into the slow procession down *Calle La Paz*, hail started to fall and fall and *fall* until the gutters and streets began to fill with icy mountains, the bride's nagging suspicion that we should *not* be getting married was immediately confirmed.

Coats appeared from nowhere to cover the bride and black-suited groom, cars sped towards the church with no regard for traffic laws or pedestrians, children screamed as floral decorations on all the cars were demolished by the downpour of ice and flew off in the wake of the caravan; but the old timers immediately murmured that it was a sign of good fortune because the hail was so rare an occurrence. I can testify that the hail was indeed an auspicious event given the blessings we have experienced in our married life—although the gaffes and blunders during the wedding and reception might have made us think otherwise.

In a rural town of twenty-thousand founded in the late 1500's by one of Cortez' captains, the Church and its rituals ingratiates itself into the familial lives of everyone, and so weddings are times to pause, celebrate, light fireworks and rockets, hope to be invited to the food and music of the reception, and drink to excess for as long as the bottles are full. Our soggy contingent of soon-to-be-marrieds, family, and friends arrived at the hand-cut, five-hundred year old stone courtyard of the once Augustinian monastery, now Plateresque cathedral, and on time the rain and hail stopped, a hoard of street-children flocked around the wedding party, we lined up like criminals to their execution, and the two innocents walked in hand-in-hand to their fate.

Of course, a wedding is not for the marrying couple: it is a ceremony for the public to acknowledge and affirm someone's passage in life. Looking back at the VHS tape, it's difficult not to laugh or feel chagrined at the deadpan expressions on the bride and groom, the groom botching the vows in Spanish when the priest thrusts the microphone in his face, the never-before-heard-of-in-church mariachi band playing ecclesiastical music, all the lights in the church suddenly blacking out for several minutes while the ceremony idles in neutral, Elvira's giggling nieces putting the huge rosary-like lasso around each of our necks with its obvious symbolism, the placing of the thirteen old silver peso's in her diminutive hands, and the awkward kiss in front of hundreds of gawking townspeople who knew neither of us.

We fled the church and greeted well-wishers outside until we could take it no longer. Elvira's perfectionist brother led us to his pickup truck and whisked us away to El Salon Alegria Chinoy, the reception hall he had booked for the five-hundred or so guests already pouring in from the tiny surrounding mountain communities of Parangarito, San Miguel El Alto, El Granjenal, Ochomitas, La Tinaja, and Tierra Blanca (where Elvira was born in a twelve-foot square brick cabin). Our arrival at the non-descript, cement block building triggered head-turning and murmuring among the hundreds of people already seated at the fold-out tables waiting for the bored waiters to hurry up and bring the alcohol. The most colorfully dressed mariachi group started up with "*El Gustito*," and the desultory crowd shifted in their chairs and looked to see if the gringo would carry his *novia* into the salon. It turned out to be the only time I lifted up this petite spitfire; she felt it was degrading while I felt it was chivalrous, one of our many cultural conflicts. I managed not to trip over the train of her dress as I followed fingers pointing to two folding chairs directly behind the three-layer cake that obscured our view throughout the entire evening.

As soon as we sat, the rock group started up with "*La Bamba*," and soon everyone was struggling to dance first to the Mexican rock music, the mariachi, then rock, mariachi, then rock, until the rock group eventually yielded to the superior force of the six mariachi trumpets. Waiters finally began serving rum and coke, platters of carnitas, rice, beans; and baskets of tortillas with beautifully embroidered napkins folded over them were placed here and there on each table, while guests who knew the family well came over to shake our hands and express their good wishes (as far as my intermediate Spanish could determine). Elvira's mother and father arrived and took their place next to us, and then a cavalcade of brothers in their elaborate *charro* suits and wide-brimmed hats with their wives all overdressed in brocade sheath dresses came in to take their places in descending order of age.

When a family brother-in-law barber who had a head start on drinking leaned over in front of me and asked what song I wanted to hear, I was at a loss for titles, so I settled on the obvious "*Guadalajara.*" Little did I know the mariachis would sing the off-color, racy verses about pubic hair, which brought howls of laughter from everyone including the children who were running around everywhere at top speed amped up on Coca-cola and the loud music. I made a speech in Spanish about how wonderful it was to have cultural exchange through marriage, we offered a toast of hard cider to Elvira's family and the town, we cut the cake and smashed small pieces into each other's face trying to smile about such a stupid custom while everyone else cheered and waited politely for their paper plate of cake.

When everyone else had been served, we obligingly danced the first waltz wondering out loud when we would have to leave to make our plane connection two hours away in Mexico City for our honeymoon in *Isla Mujeres,* the little island off the coast of Cancun. But next came the "*Vibora del Mar,*" where two rickety chairs are placed three feet apart from each other, and on one stands the bride, and on the other the groom holding her veil up like an arch. All the women, *all the women,* young, old, ponderous, sexy, arthritic, athletic, available, and taken hold hands and dance like a weaving snake under the veil. That was fun. Then the money dance where she and I dance as if we don't know what's happening, and people come up goofy and embarrassed to stuff paper money into her...wherever...bodice, waistband, cuff, hair band, you name it. We made off with fifteen hundred pesos and change, well worth the embarrassment.

When everyone had eaten their fill of carnitas, beans, and rice, the second round of bottles was brought to all the tables, and dancing between men and women, women and women, girls and girls, and girls and boys began in earnest. Elvira's brother, Roberto, caught my eye, nodded towards the door and nodded again. With a word to her mother and father, we walked one after the other out the door to the parking lot as if we were going to greet a new set of arrivals and be right back. We stuffed ourselves into his red Datsun pickup, drove to her parents' house, changed into travelling clothes, threw our four suitcases in the back of the camper, asked her brother why grinning sixteen-year old Lito, her nephew, was ensconced in the back of the camper shell and not in the front seat riding shotgun with her brother, then realized we would have another chaperone with us evidently protecting my wife's maidenhood from the lecherous white man. Too late.

On the bumpy, uncomfortable ride to the airport little Lito dozed on one side of Elvira while I, on the other side, let my mind and hands wander where they would while trying not to awaken and perhaps scandalize the innocent boy. The rain dripping incessantly directly on our heads from the leaking roof of the dilapidated camper shell was just the thing for cooling our ardor, and it prevented us from napping or from much else except complaining on the two-hour drive from Yuriria to Mexico City. In spite of the uncomfortable and frustrating situation, we were on the way to our honeymoon, and not even Lito, the potholes and bumps, nor the rain could dampen our excitement to be free of chaperones and act like the newlyweds we finally were.

Chapter 11: Helluva Honeymoon

"I smell the steamy sweat of Eros and seduction and feel dark desires for the lascivious and the forbidden. Each and every fruit demands a kiss and irresistibly intoxicates my mind. I breathe in lust and exhale bold passion...My soul I had considered sound and stable takes flight and rises with a thousand winds. I grow boundless and dissolve in this lustrous cosmos united with the world."
Hermann Hesse
"Dreaming of Paradise" 1926

This may surprise you, but I'm wondering why you have not included something on sex as a form of prayer. (I) wonder if it might not help everybody to bring prayer and sex into closer relationship. Would your book possibly be a good place to do that? I'd really like to hear your feeling about that. [lix]
Brother Paul Williams

Isla de Las Mujeres

I REMEMBER NOTHING about arriving at the airport in the murky dusk of Mexico City after the 2 hour drive from our wedding reception in Yuriria; nothing about trying to unfold our cramped selves and Lito and luggage from the uncomfortable and soggy bed of Roberto's rickety red Datsun pickup; nothing about the chaos inside the world's largest airport with tickets and customs and the stupid button you push to get a red or green light for customs opening or not opening your luggage; nothing about the holding-hands, romantic flight or pray-to-God landing at the airport outside Cancun; nothing about the sweaty taxi ride to Puerto Juarez where the ferry supposedly would take us over to the then luxurious Hotel *Presidente*; and nothing about the 10 minute, bouncy, I'm-going-to-throw-up-with-the-smell-of-gasoline fishing skiff ferry ride to the Island of the Women.

What I do recall vividly and with detail as we skimmed over the gem-like turquoise water is approaching the small island and catching sight of several women wading knee-deep in the shallow water around the hotel beach area, blond Anglo women, that is, all proudly displaying their genetic assets by jumping up and down, frolicking topless with each other to the delight of a score of young native men who had pulled their tiny boats in an appropriately wide yet tight circle around the area and were calling out to the exhibitionist ladies what I assumed but couldn't confirm were propositions that their wives or girlfriends had probably turned down ages ago.

"Do you see that?" My sweet ingenuous wife elbowed me and nodded her head in the direction of the quickly approaching spectacle of bobbling bosoms.

"Of course, I see that, Honey," and I added innocently, "but I'm not actually looking at them…"

"You mean at those women?"

"Of course not!"

"Oh, you mean you're looking at their boobs?"

"Well, not at their boobs either, Honey."

"They're big, aren't they?"

"You mean their boobs?"

"Of course, I mean their boobs," she was sounding indignant, "do you think I mean the women themselves."

"Well, they are pretty big, aren't they?" I had noticed quickly that all the women were rather tall and big-boned, Germanic-looking specimens of womanhood.

"See, I knew you were looking at their boobs."

The leering captain of the boat slowed to a crawl as we passed five women who were splashing water on each other and displaying their treasures from every angle. He steered the little boat close enough so that the tanned mermaids began splashing the captain without any thought for his passengers. He doffed his San Francisco Giants cap in their direction and yelled out something in Spanish I did not understand, but my stern-faced wife jabbed me in the ribs again and informed me we would not be coming here again. Later that afternoon the desk clerk informed us that German tourists in particular came here to vacation, and the hotel staff wouldn't stop the women from going topless because they tipped so lavishly at the bar.

We checked in to the air-conditioned, lime green and cream swirled marble floored hotel, took the elevator up to our fifth-floor room along with the bellboy who was struggling with our four overstuffed bags, found the room that overlooked the crystalline turquoise water, and once in the room, we flopped down on the bed and slept for several hours without even unpacking. We woke suddenly and began laughing out loud—about the spectacle of the topless women, about the fact that we were finally there alone with no chaperones, and about the fact that we had each brought two extra particularly heavy, over-packed bags with us filled with what we thought were invaluable treasures we would be needing every day on our honeymoon.

Elvira had one bag exclusively devoted to shoes—her beloved Petite Jeans high heels from the boutiques of Morelia and Mexico City, her silver and pearl encrusted Cinderella heels from the wedding, incredibly pointy black stiletto heels totally incongruous for a girl from a tiny town in the breadbasket of Mexico but very sexy, sandals of all types, penny loafers, Addidas tennis shoes, and generic flip-flops. All in all we counted twenty-six pairs of shoes for all occasions stuffed carefully in her bag. We laugh regularly at the fact that she only wore two pair of shoes during the entire honeymoon, one pair of sandals and one modest pair of heels, but most of time we were blissfully shoeless in the warm Caribbean water and in bed, of course.

I was even more the subject of our lightheartedness. I had packed my second grip with boxes and bags of Mexican candy that I had procured at the Disneyland-like candy stores in Yuriria, a temptation for every candy-lover. I was ashamedly afraid that if I had left the candy in her house in Yuriria, all of Elvira's nieces and nephews would have helped themselves, and there would have been nothing left for the newly married couple, strike that, I mean me, sweet-toothed and greedy me. I had carefully chosen bags of hard candies, Carlos Quinto chocolate bars, candy with cardamom seeds hidden inside, anise flavored candy, chocolate and marshmallow candies, candy made with the caramel-like *cajeta*, coconut candies, candies made from fruit jellies, and candy made from the fruit pod, tamarindo, some with chile, some with salt, some with sugar, all pucker-producing.

Neither of us had ever traveled far from home before our honeymoon, a couple of Rubes, Oh, God!, and to this day we relish travel adventures together where we discover something about the people there and something about ourselves we can laugh and hug about. Our travel adventures are now pared down each to one of those small, black, boxy, canvas suitcases: we know what we really need when we travel, and that is each other. The sharing of adventure together creates opportunities to see oneself and each other in a new light, and the new situations create tiny opportunities for bonding—I hate that word—change it to team-building, no…that's not it either. It's just times when both of us can go through a mini-adventure or challenge, put our heads together, and move forward with some kind of direction or solution that might matter or not, times when we can choose a little restaurant, order something, and enjoy the surprise of food that someone else makes that makes us grow together in the small victories and be able to look back with some nostalgia and humor augmented and burnished by time and the fact that we are still married and in love.

So, this was our honeymoon on *Isla Mujeres*, island of the women, Yeeesss! Our second goal while there was to visit every little restaurant big and small to sample and evaluate the different versions of shrimp cocktail and chicken soup. It was on that search that we discovered the world's most refreshing soda, available only in Mexico, Crystal de Piña, a crystal-clear pineapple soda colored the most synthetically chartreuse color imaginable, yet, when chilled to almost freezing, it washes down those hurriedly chewed pieces of shrimp and chicken and cools down any hot salsa or chile peppers you might have added to the cocktail or soup out of habit (if you're Mexican) or to get a little additional punch or cachet (if your Anglo). We visited at least ten eateries, some with only two rickety folding tables and chairs, and some with rows of tables and booths covered with Carta Blanca place mats, and there was not one in which we found shrimp cocktail or chicken soup that we did not enjoy.

The best shrimp cocktail, of course, is one with whole shrimp, eyes, and feelers, including the shell. The most delectable flavors are contained in the yummy "mustard" or "tamale" inside the head savored by foodies on both sides of the border. A shrimp cocktail should also have the right balance of juiciness (from Clamato, tomato, or V-8 juice), sweetness (from a dash of catsup, never sugar), fire (from some form of chile), crunch (from chopped celery and celery leaves, thinly sliced cabbage, cucumber, and/or green onion), flavor (from cilantro, black pepper perhaps, and lemon juice), and a little warm togetherness from sliced or cubed ripe avocado. There you have a memorable shrimp cocktail, assuming the shrimp is fresh and "deveined"—a wonderfully useful and humorous euphemism. Serve with lemon slices and perhaps a little bottle of local salsa, my preference for shrimp cocktail being chipotle Tabasco sauce.

The schedule of our honeymoon on the island repeated itself daily.

1. Wake up late after cavorting in each other's arms (or other variations of "in each other's arms").

2. I actually cannot remember what we did next until lunch time when we broached daylight to stumble the couple blocks into town to try the next shrimp cocktail and chicken soup adventure.

3. Walk around town just to see the sights.

4. Return to hotel room, cavort wildly on the ample sill of the huge window overlooking the vast expanse of the Caribe, and try not to break what was most certainly not tempered glass.

5. Go wading, splashing, kissing, and spacing out in the invitingly stunning and warm turquoise ocean.

6. Go swimming in the cool hotel pool strategically located next to the swim-up tequila bar.

7. Drink tequila while in the pool, and talk with other tequila drinkers from Canada and Mexico who were undoubtedly in the pool on a similar schedule.

8. Go upstairs to the hotel room, shower, cavort on the bed this time, sleep the sleep of babies. Awaken. Repeat.

9. Walk into town, see the sights, have a snack (tacos, enchiladas, a Negra Modelo, Carta Blanca, for variety).

10. Watch the sun set while kissing and hugging.

11. Repeat #8.

12. Imprint all this in long-term memory to laugh and cry over years later when Elvira and I are not in Mexico.

The Hotel *Presidente*—in those days the most luxurious hotel on the island, nowadays barely showing up on a Google search of "hotels *isla mujeres*"—was way expensive at two-fifty a night, so the bride and groom decided to change to a little run-down-at-the-edges but charming hotel, *Maria del Mar*. This welcoming little gem was closer to town and right on the beach where the pool was almost hot, where the housekeeper washed and ironed the groom's shirts in a couple hours, and where we had breakfasts and dinners on the beach under a rustic little pergola made from driftwood, shells, and fishing nets. So the naive travelers lugged their four still-bulging bags across the quarter mile of burning pavement from The *Presidente* to *Maria del Mar*. The marks the straps imprinted in our shoulders remained for several hours, and it was only in looking back across the burning pavement we had just walked that we saw taxis we could have taken for a few pesos. We saw no reason to laugh then, but mutual self-deprecating humor bubbles up now when we recall such comical moments.

The next morning breakfast plates of tiny *pan dulces*, scrambled eggs with chorizo, cheek-soft hand-made tortillas, a pot of strong coffee, and fresh orange juice rejuvenated us for more schedule-keeping. Huge prawns wrapped with bacon, Mexican rice, and fresh vegetables sautéed with chiles, and beer rounded out dinner. The soft breeze of the evening soothed us as it rolled in from over the transparent azure ocean. (I had to write that hackneyed sentence because in this case it was so true.) We slept under mosquito netting in a non-air-conditioned room, and there were no chaperones to tell us we were or were not having the most wonderful honeymoon anyone could imagine.

Contoy Island

The next morning (I am guessing) we were down at the dock to sign on to the rock 'n' rolling boat trip to Contoy Island, an animal sanctuary ten miles from *Isla*. We climbed into the high-prowed outboard fishing boat and discovered two more passengers on the trip with us. In the bow section of the boat two young women in their late twenties early thirties were chatting gaily, gesticulating animatedly, exposing now and then brown thickets of armpit hair I had never imagined could exist or ever witnessed on the body of any woman I had ever been close to. Flaunting their armpit bush is a more accurate description of their liberated exhibition. They were displaying their liberation, freedom, sensitivity, and acceptance of real life by means of their armpit hair. Elvira and I turned a surreptitious glance at each other, and I wondered if she was curious too if they were going to flash their nether bushes too for good measure. I was glad though they never did. When I realized they were speaking French, I thought secretly, *Oh, yeah, French women...I wonder...*

Twenty minutes into the bone-jarring, high-speed charge out to Contoy Island, the captain (a Mexican guy wearing a Hobie surfing bathing suit and flip-flops) slowed then stopped suddenly.

"You dive here?" he looked at each of us and raised his black eyebrows.

"Sure!" I blurted out not thinking I should run such a ludicrous idea by my wife before going over the side.

"What are you going to do, Chas?" She asked—assaulted me verbally actually—as I pulled on two huge swimming fins.

"You know I love swimming, Honey," I replied in a neutral tone hoping to calm her natural tendency to freak out. "I'll be fine, the water's really clear, and you know, I *am* a Pisces. I'll be right back, Baby," I added as I rolled over the side into the warm water.

I treaded water, adjusted the snorkel, took a couple deep breaths, and plunged down into the crystalline water. I thought I heard Elvira squeal in a high voice, "shark," but I ignored it in my preoccupation to descend quickly to the bottom. Schools of tropical fish zoomed across my field of view, some right across my face—

blue, yellow, white, and black fish, all shaped like torpedoes, some blunt, some thin, all swimming in the protective field of their schools. My lungs began to burn, and I shot up the twenty or so feet to the surface where I was immediately met with Elvira agitatedly calling over the side, "The captain says there's sharks down there. Get up here right now, Honey!"

I was down again before she finished her apprehensive suggestion so I could act as if I hadn't heard her. I saw several bullet-like barracuda but no sharks. I reveled in the underwater beauty while the other world slowed down, magnified, and heightened by the clear three-dimensional window of seawater. I've never passed up the opportunity to dive into the ocean, and being a Pisces with my sun and moon in Pisces (whatever that means), I am always at home in water, the most so in the ocean.

I dove four or five times before the captain said, "*Ya vamonos*," and I pulled my elated self back up into the boat where my dear wife berated me for having such a great time at her expense. The captain confirmed that this was indeed a shark feeding area, and I thanked him for not telling me before I went down. My dear wife pointed out that, while I had been cavorting irresponsibly in the water, the captain had been fishing for our lunch and had pulled in two three foot barracuda, the same kind of barracuda that have many many razor sharp teeth. *Oh-kay...Those were the long torpedo shaped fish I thought were so graceful and all?*

"See! I told you so, Honey, you don't listen to me, do you?" She asked me rhetorically as the two French ladies smiled politely with their arms courteously at their sides.

"I had a great time down there, Baby! I love it!"

"You didn't see any sharks down there?"

"Of course not, there's no sharks down there regardless of what *el capitan* said."

The captain pulled the cord, the ancient outboard roared to life, and we took off again, the small boat rising up on each swell then crashing down with a huge splash that inundated the two Frenchies every three seconds or so. We spied Contoy Island after ten minutes of holding on to the gunwales of the lurching, bouncing boat, and the captain slowed to give us a view of the entire circumference of the island. We weren't close enough to see if they were crocs or alligators, but the captain assured us that there were lots of them. Huge sea birds nesting in the mangroves. Dolphins cruising slowly in clusters. Large pleasure boats from the mainland anchored here and there. It is an isolated oasis where only peculiar creatures lurk.

We tied up at a small wharf on the lee side of the island alongside a huge white luxury cabin cruiser named "Pura Vida" off which crew members were carrying boxes and boxes of food, beer, champagne, and tables and chairs. A well-tanned, wrinkled, but well-hung tomcat in a red thong with a full wine glass in one hand and another pointing here and there were both directing other crew members where and how to set up the picnic on the wide beach areas by the pier. Elvira pointed out appropriately how plump the man's derriere appeared, how uncomfortable the thong must have been given the fact it had disappeared between his buttocks, and how embarrassed he must have been showing off his equipment that way.

"That is some heavy-duty machinery, for sure, Honey, I would be proud of it, not embarrassed."

Now and then Elvira turned to inspect the situation in the rear as we debarked onto the pier accompanied by the two giggling French girls, our captain, and the two dispatched barracuda. The captain proceeded to build a rustic fire on the beach, then he scaled, gutted, and filleted the two beautiful fish. He spread a red spice mixture on the fish, put them directly on the burned-down coals, and prodded them here and there until he was satisfied. We ate rich fish tacos doused with lemon juice and bottled salsa, and we washed it down with Negra Modelo that the captain produced from a hidden ice chest. I raised my eyebrows humorously when I caught Elvira affirming again that the full-fannied beefcake was still there suffering from thong strangulation.

The effete travelers had already descended from their yacht and were ensconced on the beach in lawn chairs around several tables set with glassware, cloth napkins, bottles in champagne buckets, and plates of what appeared to be fruit and sandwiches. The bikinied stud was accompanied by several other well-equipped sexy sweating examples of languorous masculinity. Several young and lithe appearing over-tanned women looked bored and out-of-place, and they made up for their malaise by kissing each other on the mouth, laughing uproariously in Spanish laced with what even I could tell was sexual innuendo, and drinking champagne from the open bottles they pulled from the ice buckets. Nouveau riche from Mexico City, I thought. Creeps!

We waded in the shallow water as far from the partiers as we could while the captain cleaned up from lunch. As I waded out up to mid-knee, several manta rays glided in stealthily to the clear sandy shallows. They bumped ever so slightly into my shins and calves as they moved gracefully past me as if to say, "Remember that this is our domain, but we will let you share it for a while." Elvira noticed and rushed out of the water screaming, "They're going to sting you! Get out of the water, Honey!" The captain heard the ruckus, hurried over, and mentioned too casually for Elvira that if I just walked slowly out of the water without splashing they wouldn't cause any harm. I did as he said and survived another attack from vicious sea creatures, thank God.

On the trip back to the dock at *Isla* Elvira and I were preoccupied, this time not with the armpit hair of our fellow travelers, but with keeping her from falling over the side of the boat as she heaved up the barracuda, salsa, tortillas, and beer into the Pacific Ocean. We all held on for dear life as we crested each swell head on then slammed down into the deep trough with a huge splash that sent water into the boat soaking all four passengers and captain to the bone.

"*Agárense duro*," shouted the captain over the sound of the motor and waves. There was no need to suggest that we all hold on tight because we were already doing that to save our lives. My dear Elvira had finally had enough of watching the ocean pass a foot from her face, so the remainder of the trip back was more unpleasant than adventuresome, particularly since the last twenty minutes of bouncing and slamming into the water became the perfect opportunity to learn that the trip to Contoy Island was completely my idea, and a stupid idea at that. *I'm sorry, Honey. How could I have thought of such a stupid thing for us to do?*

After three days of following the paradise of our honeymoon schedule, we decided to take the bus, yes, I said, *"take the bus,"* over 300 kilometers from Cancun across the thin jungled peninsula, to Mérida, the ancient capital of Mexico. It was bad enough that neither of us had ever traveled farther than a day's radius from home; it was even worse that we did not seem to know or recall the difference between an express and a local bus, so when the concierge at the *Presidente* eagerly presented us with two tickets on the *Primera Plus* bus line the next morning to Merida, I tipped him generously without knowing that that damn bus would stop in every little vestige of Mayan town along the way to Valladolid, the original colonial capital.

Mérida

After an hour and a half, the bus wheeled through a maze of constricted side streets into the already full parking lot of the totally uncolonial bus station in Valladolid where we were met by several dirty and unkempt elderly women scooting around on their knees pulling at our sleeves begging for whatever one might give them. *On their knees.* Four other busses were leaving momentarily, we needed to go to the bathroom which seemed more like a wallow for pigs, and neither of us knew which bus to take to Mérida, so we trusted Elvira's Spanish, pulled ourselves and our burdens up on a bus that was already standing-room-only, and smiled weakly when people packed around us gave us the "You are on the wrong bus, Gringo-idiot-married-to-that-beautiful-Mexican-woman" look.

Elvira was hopelessly constipated bouncing, grimacing, and complaining all the way from Cancun from I don't know how many coconut popsicles she ate in *Isla*. We sped by Chitzén Itza silently grateful that we were not going to stop and climb the pyramids there, and the driver ground down into first to coast by scores of little Mayan villages with names like Yaxche and Hoctun where naked children and dogs played in the highway. We finally pulled into Mérida in a driving warm tropical rainstorm, without a guidebook, without hotel reservations, carrying those damned four heavy bags two of which were still stuffed full of sexy high heels and a generous assortment of Mexican candy. Two rubes we were. Meant for each other, remember?

We stepped down off the bus into a wide gutter flowing with muddy water. Elvira tripped and fell in the dirty water, cursed in wonderfully surprising vulgar Spanish, and in exasperation threw her colorful, wide-brim, hand-made straw hat I had just bought her in *Isla Mujeres* high up into the air. The sombrero sailed across the street and landed in the gutter full of chaotic rainwater, and my sweet bride expressed her sentiments again in her native language.

"Maldita ciudad!" I had never heard her curse a city before, but on a honeymoon a lot of things happen for the first time.

Taxis were not moving in the downpour, and even drivers we promised to pay double refused to take us to shelter. We turned our back on the hat floating forlornly down the gutter and struggled along the sidewalk hugging the wall in the direction the bus driver pointed out as prime hotel territory. Every ten feet we had to drop our precious bags, stop and catch our breath, argue without attracting attention about whether we were having a fun honeymoon or not, then pick up the soggy bags, and struggle on until after ten minutes of protracted walking, stumbling, and whispering, we suddenly came upon the hotel we assumed the driver had mentioned.

An old colonial three story home, grand and elegant in its time, tarnished rococo gold gilt, wide sagging mezzanines circling each floor overlooking the empty fountain of broken lime green marble in the center of the first floor, loose wooden louvered doors on each room with locks that didn't function, hot water two hours a day in the morning, beds that sagged more than our backs were capable of enduring, and little noise during the evening because we were the only guests there. It was clear why that was.

Mérida is a beautiful relic of colonial grandeur with the mundane and the surprising at every turn of the head. A mysterious darkly lit passageway where we found an old Mayan woman's floral treasures spread out on a small woven blanket set onto the dark stained cobblestones of the alley floor— calla lilies of all colors, riotously colored bromeliads, fragrant gardenias and nard flowers, sprigs of purple jacaranda, all colors of orchids large and small from her jungle Eden, stems covered with Mexican orange blossoms, so many other flowers we did not recognize or have to time to ask the name because we were on our way to another adventure. Several minutes later we realized that *that* was what we had come to Merida for, and when we tried to return to that obscure little lane to buy more flowers and listen to the old woman's eyes speak, we could not find the alley or her again. It was as if she had never been there although we were carrying the flowers she had wrapped in the newspaper cornucopia for us. We carried the flowers with us for what must have been weeks until they dried, shriveled, and left only their scent behind like this memory of that old woman's beautiful offerings.

For three days we slept the dreamless sleep at night and roamed the streets during the daytime following our noses with a mutual nod of assent to turn into this street or that building. One senses the layers of life that have accumulated in old cities, particularly metropolitan crossroads where cultures have replaced cultures either by the sword, by trade, or by time. The Catholic cathedrals of Mexico are the perfect palimpsest—constructed from the limestone blocks ravaged by conquistadors from Aztec and Mayan temples and pyramids, the same blocks cut by Aztec and Mayan slaves—culture synthesized by force like genetic engineering, gene splicing, religious fundamentalism, or modern politics.

We roamed the streets of Mérida like one would meander the hidden streams and glens of a lover's body, straying here and there where the shadows and smells emanating from within pulled us in wordlessly, drifting with the currents of passion that closed our eyes to fear or timidity when the earth moved imperceptivity, giving our curiosity free rein to uncover the layers of that still throbbing world and lay down the iridescent nacre of our own eagerness and joy to be together where we had never been. These are secrets unable to be shared with others for they have no referents, and so those mysterious surprises would mean no more than if I wrote, "We had an incredible time in Mérida."

Road Food

A two-engine commuter flew us back to Mexico City where Elvira's older sister, Gracia, and her husband, Elias, picked us up in their red compact pick-up. They had five days of vacation to show us around their Mexico.

"We're going to take you to Acapulco!"

The photos show us riding in the back of the tiny truck like we were on a buckin' bronc, Elvira in her bikini standing up leaning  forward with her hair streaming out behind her in the warm mountain air, me grinning like a frog in mud because I was married to this angel. For breakfast we stopped for beer and soda, splayed chicken roasted over charcoal and served with sliced avocados and hot salsa made from roasted tomatoes, chiles, onion, and garlic. An hour later Elias pulled over for lunch at the top of a mountain pass, and both he and Gracia said there was a special recipe we were going to try that was served only there.

"What's so special about this place?" Both Elvira and I asked, seeing that it was just a tiny, non-descript, grimy concrete block building with one wooden table outside.

"Well, they make freshwater langoustino here with a recipe that is rumored to be an aphrodisiac, at least we heard that..."

They caught each other's eye and raised their eyebrows knowingly while we stretched our legs and backs and started to walk across the dirt parking area to the grungy building. The small langoustino were fresh, roasted over wood coals, with a marinade we discussed heatedly as we sucked the luscious meat from the shells, took bites of the ripe avocados, and swiped salsa from the paper plates with the homemade corn tortillas.

"It's gotta be cloves and cinnamon, maybe cumin too..."

"Of course, cumin, you know what they say about cumin..."

"They roasted garlic too before they used it, it's sweet..."

"We'll see what happens later, eh?" Everyone laughed with our mouths full.

The four of us ate our fill, at least a dozen of those sweet hand-size crustaceans, without any thought of cost, waistlines, or after-effects. We drove another fifty miles through mist covered mountains, Elvira and I shivering but dry in the back of the pick-up with our heads poking out of black plastic garbage bags, winding over the heavily forested mountains of pine, cedar, and spruce until Elias pulled off at another mountaintop parking area.

"Rabbit!" He turned and whispered out the rear window of the cab.

"We just ate an hour ago, Elias," I replied.

"Yeah, but you haven't eaten rabbit cooked over cedar wood, have you?"

I had to admit that I hadn't, and very soon we were tearing into halves of succulent rabbit that had been marinated with garlic, fresh oregano, and marjoram and cooked to falling-off-the-bones. We chuckled when we noticed a vintage Caddy pull in, a woman got out hurriedly and rush over to our table, then turned, obviously disgruntled and put out because, as we heard her vehemently announce to us in Spanish,

"What kind of rundown dump is this where they don't even have forks or knives to eat with?"

She looked back directly at us and added, "This is only for poor people who have no manners or money to pay for real food."

We shook our heads as she tromped off to the car while we relished one of the best meals I have ever eaten, tearing off juicy, smoky smelling, cedar-barbequed rabbit with soft homemade tortillas, cramming our mouths full of simple yet luxurious food.

Dusk had crept in by the time we arrived in Chilpancingo, their home, the infamous mountain town where they both struggled to organize local workers to conserve the abundant forest resources rather than slashing and cutting the hillsides. Other more profit-minded farmers planted thousands of hectares of marijuana, the same marijuana that incites gang wars over turf and profit, the same marijuana that eventually finds its way to the US where it travels from hand to hand until it ends up rolled into a joint a high schooler pulls out of her purse or his wallet at lunch, lights up, and passes around. We fell into bed that night, faces sunburned from a day in the back of the truck bed, stuffed with food of the gods, with aches and bruises from bouncing over the roads, and with the desperate need to sleep.

The prediction about the after-effects of the langoustino proved accurate, and Elvira and I were constantly worried that the noise of the huge hardwood bed scraping and banging on the tile floor would keep Gracia and Elias awake.

"Did you get any sleep last night?" was their sheepish first question the next morning over coffee.

"Uh, I think we did," I answered diplomatically while looking to Elvira for help.

"We're not stopping at that place again!" She blurted out, and that was the end of it.

They had less than three more days to show the newlyweds around the Mexico they knew from their work with the *campesinos*, with the forests, with the Monarch butterflies, and then deliver us back to Elvira's home town unscathed. The Acapulco they showed us is overshadowed and hidden by the 1950's mansions jutting out or clinging tenaciously to the steep cliffs, the newer-than-new contemporary estates cut into the hillsides and conspicuously pretentious and over-the top even for rich Mexicans; and we passed by the glitz and sparkle of the beach attractions—the hotels, the bars, discos, the four and five star restaurants.

We checked into the most claustrophobic, stuffy, and noisy budget motel imaginable with convoluted stairwells and hallways, faded light green paint that reeked of fifty-year old cigarette smoke, and parking spaces that would only accommodate a Mini-Cooper. Fortunately we spent the entire day at Puerto Marquez southeast of Acapulco itself, a cozy little beach, too steep for walking, but perfect for sitting under umbrellas stuck in the sand in front of little food stalls where already well-fed women were sliding rolled chicken and ground beef taquitos into sizzling oil and then fishing them out to put on the endless plates the adolescent boy waiters would hurry to the shade of your umbrella along with buckets of ice packed with Negra Modelo, Carta Blanca, Bohemia, or whatever brand of beer you fancied. We ordered, ate and drank, napped in the ocean air, called the waiter again, ordered something different from the cook, repeated the deep fried excess, slept more, then woke up and decided it was time for dinner.

The weather reports for the following few days became more and more ominous the further out the reports went, so we decided to hightail it back to Yuriria so as not to get caught in any thunder, hail, or lightning storms given the continuing fact that Elvira and I were riding in the rumble seat. The closer we got to our destination the more raingear we put on—first the usual large plastic garbage bags, then as it got colder, sweatshirts under the garbage bags, then finally, as frightfully close lightning bolts began to light up the night sky, we crammed ourselves into the cab of the tiny Japanese pickup with Elias driving, Gracia in the middle straddling the gearshift handle manipulated appropriately by her husband, then I next to the door with my dear wife properly on my lap. No seat belts: this is Mexico. No windshield wipers: I had the long arms and a towel. No heater: everyone was shivering and no one complained. My legs had fallen asleep hours before, and my bladder was beyond the point of bursting.

Full Circle

As we pulled into the convoluted streets of Yuriria that night, the clouds we thought had already dumped all their rain on us let go and drenched the entire area and lit up the entire nightscape with the most other-worldly lightening I had ever witnessed. When we pulled up in front of 21 La Paz, Elvira's Mexican home, we all got out, but Elias stayed in the car with the motor idling. As Gracia took a few moments to talk with him, Elvira clued me to one of the family...uh, scandals, no, situations, yes, that's more diplomatic, situation. Let's put it this way:

> *Once upon a time there was a princess most favored by her father, the king. Upon her shoulders he lavished the best education; freedom most women did not even imagine; the esteem of all royalty; the possession of and skill with horses and weapons; and all hopes for the future of the royal family and the country. While she was across the sea*

studying and training for the day she would become queen, she fell in love with a prince from that far away realm. She discovered very soon that he had two children in secret with a common lass whom he had cast off and disallowed. The princess knew her father, the king, would never ever allow her to marry a prince who had children, and with a wench like that, so she devised an ingenious plan by which she and the prince could be married, a plan that only a princess that intelligent and that bold could carry out.

The princess sent messages to her father, the king, and her mother, the queen, to the effect that she would send her husband-to-be back over the sea to her home where he would meet her father and mother, help prepare the wedding festivities, and wait for her arrival at which time they would be married. Yet the princess being more clever than all, knew her father would not allow the wedding and might even kill the prince on first sight. So the princess sent the prince's most trusted manservant to represent the prince at the wedding telling the king and queen that he would be her true husband.

The manservant was comely, gentle, magnanimous, and courteous, and he impressed everyone who met him. They were married on the appointed day with the king and queen beaming with happiness at their daughter's marriage with such a wonderful prince. When night after night the princess refused to take to the marriage bed high in the castle, the king and queen thought it strange, but they gave it no mind because the newlywed couple seemed so content, so happy, and so perfect for each other.

It was only when the princess sent her legal husband, the prince's manservant, back overseas on a diplomatic mission, and then announced a month later that he had been killed in a tragic shipwreck, that the prince himself was able to arrive and claim his true love. He arrived on the evening tide, announced his true love for the princess, and they were married after a suitable period of mourning for her manservant/husband.

Life and people being what and who they are, the king and queen discovered that they had been duped, lied to, and played the fool by their only precious daughter, the princess. They commanded that the prince never be allowed to enter the castle or any family residence in the kingdom. The daughter was stripped of her title and inheritance. The princess and prince were relegated to the status of commoner, and that is how they remain to this day. Little is left of the princess's audacity and insensitivity. It is known among many inhabitants of the kingdom, but no one speaks of it out of consideration for the poor prince.

And so that is why Elvira whispered in my ear that blustery cold and windy night that Elias would not be coming into the shelter of the family home, but instead would be turning that tiny cold truck around without even a bathroom stop and driving back all night alone through the thunderstorm of his making to Chilpancingo. An odd thing it is that I—also "with two children in secret with a common lass whom I had cast off and disallowed"—I am the most accepted and respected of all the men and women who have married into the king and queen's family. Another one of life's charming ironies it is.

Within two days Elvira and I had chatted with every relative in town about made-up events and the superficialities of our honeymoon. We dared not tell them of our adventures and the close collaboration and affinity we developed during those two weeks of loving and living together in strange and wonderful circumstances. Perhaps no newlyweds speak of their true honeymoon. Perhaps all newlyweds grow close, so very close, like we did on our honeymoon. I am certain that is one powerful reason we are still married after 25 years: we still relish the shared adventure of living, most of it wonderful, and the very little that is sorrowful.

We flew together out of the airport at the capital of Guanajuato, Morelia, and were home in Salinas, California that night. *The next day* my two children from my previous marriage arrived to stay for the summer.

Welcome to Wal-Mart...er... Home!

Chapter 12: Curandero's Healing

"Only now do I realize how many paths there are to knowledge and that the path of the mind is not the only one and perhaps not even the best one." [lx]
Hermann Hesse
Narcissus and Goldmund

Hope your explorations with Don Fidel were fruitful, and I look forward to hearing more whenever you care to share. Your emptiness, especially in church, is a deep and pregnant emptiness, a quiet waiting that is beautiful and powerful. Like a woman waiting to be filled with the warm seed of life. It's a feeling I know too—a good feeling—something to be cherished...I love the way you have dealt with your family... The development into the loving family that you have is extraordinarily powerful, and the kind of message our world needs to hear. My deepest love to them and to you, my dear friend. [lxi]
Brother Paul Williams

WHEN THE DIVORCE WAS FINALIZED, I had the presence of mind and heart to buy a house for Elvira and me to move into. The last thing I wanted was to move her into the passive solar house I had built with my ex. The house was 5 bedroom, in a cul-de-sac, with hot tub, close to work, perfect. David and I had returned from our spirit quest, and Elvira and I had married and honeymooned in Mexico. When we returned from our south-of-the-border marriage and honeymoon, she and I faced one of the biggest challenges we have ever confronted—the vindictive ex-wife. Now, exes are always the butt of jokes, especially when the joker has suffered through the process of creating that ex. The story is often the same, particularly when the bifurcating couple has had the foresight to create children to use as unwitting and unwilling surrogates in the judo tournament for power and righteousness. It will be illustrative here to list only a few cogent high and low points of the protracted melee rather than subject the reader to a narrative recreation of our descent into Dante's Inferno.

First.

Only a saint would accept another woman's children as her own, particularly immediately upon return from her honeymoon, and Elvira was and still is saint-like. She gave Spanish lessons every afternoon to 6 year old Miles and 7 year old Piper, something that has proven to be a true boon to both, particularly to Piper who spent three Peace Corps years off the coast of Spanish-speaking Panama on Bocas Del Toro Island helping the indigenous people develop basic sanitation and micro-economic opportunities for themselves. This very month she ventures off to Guatemala to work with micro-economic developments in that area. A gringo woman working with Guatemalan men to develop their economy? Even Miles, the maverick/non-conformist/artist member of the family, uses Spanish lyrics in his heart-felt, and unusually lyrical rap. Thank you, Elvira, you are our generous teacher.

Secondly.

Why would two step-children with lives of their own in other states want to come back and visit their wicked step-mother every year during the holidays? Because Elvira is a Mexican mother: she loves "her" children regardless of the circumstances. It helped that her father, Rafael's, mother died when he was an infant, and his father immediately married the real stereotypical step-mother who mistreated him and his brothers and sisters. He drummed into Elvira's head that she should treat her step-children with love, the love he never received. Thank you, Don Rafael, and thank you, Elvira.

Thirdly.

Who in their right minds would go to Mexico seeking a *curandero*, a *brujo*, a shaman, looking for protection from an ex intent on doing harm to the new wife? We did, and we were in our right minds in trying to protect ourselves from the poisonous, destructive, and malicious energy marshaled to harm Elvira. We found Don Fidel twenty miles outside of Cuernavaca in the primitive village of Amatlan, at the bottom of the tiny, funnel-shaped, shadowy canyon where legend has always established the birthplace of Ce Acatl, the legendary Toltec leader, later known as Topiltzin Ce Acatl Quetzacóatl, the likely historical basis of the Mesoamerican god, Quetzacóatl, the serpent-bird who created man by giving his own blood, the one who gave corn to man.

At nine in the morning there was already a line of people waiting outside Don Fidel's small rectangular concrete block hut. Next to the small house a girl was preparing tacos. The aroma of melting cheese, roasting mushrooms, nopales, and chorizo rose from her little *comál* and mixed with the sharp, rich smell of burning pine wood to fill the open space above the house with an unintended but indisputable incense that floated slowly and timelessly up past the tree tops encircling the small clearing and up even farther into the house of the gods.

Within twenty minutes Elvira and I were ushered into an intensely dark room in front of a small table. Don Fidel wore a dirty and battered straw cowboy hat, he hadn't shaved for probably a week, and he did not look up at us as he motioned for us to sit, me in front of him, and Elvira to the side.

"*Sí*," came the gruff Spanish from the dark space across from us. "Yes, I would like to read the cards for you if you would permit me. It will be my pleasure to do this because I feel there is something about you both that you need to know."

Don Fidel bowed slightly, gathered and picked up cards, Tarot cards, from the table, and as he tapped them all back into the deck, he began to rock his head and shoulders slowly back and forth while he mumbled strange and rhythmic incantations of his personal power, of ancient Nahua power, animal and earth spirit power, God-the-father-the-Son-and-the-Holy-Spirit power, the power of the saints, The Blessed Virgin Mary's power, the power of all Aztec gods, the power of Ce Acatl Topiltzin Quetzacóatl, the power of life and death, the power of dark and light spirits, woman and man power, the power of the Sun and Moon and stars and planets, the power of all people living and dead, the power of the earth beneath them, and the power that Elvira embodied there in front of him.

He shuffled and cut the deck, then dealt the cards, one after another, in an unbroken rhythm until ten cards lay before us. I had studied Don Fidel's face as he watched each card slip off the top of the deck and find its fate among the summoned and assembled pieces of our vicarious cardboard life on the table. As each card came purposefully down in its correct order and place, Don Fidel's incantations came more like a flowing river, a murmuring sibilance in which his whispered words of prayer rushed in impatiently on each inhalation and flowed out with relief on each exhalation. He would place each card down then pause momentarily just long enough to recognize it and let the significance of its nature and location add to the accretion of understanding forming across the table and in his mind.

"Uh-huh...what I thought," remarked the sorcerer without looking up at us. He studied the cards another moment or two and then looked up to find my eyes. Don Fidel leaned forward so that his upper body hovered over the cards. I felt the depth and substance of the room's darkness, and the emptiness of the small space surrounded and exposed him.

"There is a woman, a blond woman, and she is trying to kill you," Don Fidel startled me when he indicated Elvira with a slight nod of his head. "This woman is connected to you," and he nodded to me, "your wife, or she was your wife. Are you two married?"

"You, Señor, are protected from her by your shields, you know, you have power to protect yourself, did you know that? Yes, shields to protect you, but your shields must protect your wife here. What is your name, Señora?"

I took Elvira's hand as she said her name, and we both listened as Don Fidel continued to warn and instruct us.

"Your shields are weak," he turned his head to Elvira as he spoke in gruff Spanish, "but his shields," he nodded to me, "are strong, and they will protect you."

I dared not make eye contact with Elvira, but continued looking at the cards as Don Fidel continued placing them purposefully in their groups.

"There is a spider trying to poison her," he continued in Spanish as he looked up directly into my eyes. "Isn't that so?"

The *curandero* continued laying down cards thoughtfully, and as he did so, he explained the dire nature of the situation, one of life and death.

"This woman will kill you," nodding to Elvira, "if your husband does not stop her. Do you understand? I don't know exactly what I can do about this because it is between you, Señor, and your ex-wife. You are your señora's protector and teacher because you are helping her discover her own shields inside herself, and you both need protection from your ex-wife's venom."

Don Fidel pointed to the Daughter of Swords and the Daughter of Pentacles cards, how the position of the Daughter of Swords indicated power over the Daughter of Pentacles, and then explained that two other cards, The Son of Cups and the Son of Pentacles, and their positions with respect to the two Daughter cards represented me and my power and responsibility to battle my ex-wife and to protect Elvira.

"You must protect yourselves from this woman. Protect yourselves, and you will protect your wife because your shields are strong. I will bless the holy water that you will sprinkle on your doorstep...give you strong medicine...candles...anoint yourselves with this...do not let her urinate in your house..."

The whiskered curandero abruptly started to make small talk, told me that he had been in California before during the time of the braceros, that some of his sons were still in California, and then asked me if I wanted him to make a special cure to assist me. Before we could comprehend what was happening, Don Fidel stood up and was ushering us into a brilliantly lit room on the other side of the shadowy wall. In one corner a phalanx of twenty or thirty candles was burning around which were pictures and statues of the Virgin Mary and other Catholic saints, a small manger scene with the holy family and the three kings, hand carved crucifixes, bowls of water, glass jars of red and white roses, brass and silver bells, small pictures of the Aztec gods Tlaloc and Quetzacóatl, dried and preserved insects and owls and other birds, bird wings, jars of preserved scorpions, bowls of what appeared to be seeds or nuts and powders, and many large bunches of green foliage or herbs. Incense was burning furiously in several stone bowls, and the air was not air but pure pungent smoke suffused with bitter-sweet copal incense mixed with strong herbal odors.

Don Fidel motioned for me to stand by the wall, then he squatted in the corner, and I watched him pour off some liquid from a jar full of white scorpions into a drinking glass, then top it off with what the bottle said was mescal. He began chanting softly as he selected two dried roots, one white and the other grey, from assorted piles of leaves, sticks, berries, roots, beans, seeds, dead insects and other things I couldn't identify, all laid out in rows on pieces of newspaper on the floor. Don Fidel placed the roots in a large granite mortar and began to grind them slowly with a granite pestle. As he continued to mumble and grind, I noticed in an unusually perceptive way around the perimeter of the arcane pharmacopoeia the distinct and perfect owl wings, bundles of shiny black feathers, hand-carved corpuses on crucifixes, pictures of saints in poses of agony or ecstasy, rose petals floating in bowls of water, scores of bottles of different sizes and colors containing more scorpions than I thought could exist in one place all preserved in various colored liquids (such as the one I realized I would be drinking in a moment), horseshoe magnets wrapped in colored string, hundreds of thin sticks of fragrant incense, and plain and ecclesiastical candles both burning and unlit.

Don Fidel suddenly stood up, and in one continuous motion poured the powder he had ground into a small cone of paper he had formed and now held in his other hand. He picked up the glass with the mescal and God-knows-what else and quickly walked to where I still stood transfixed by what I was observing. The dark old man poured the powder into my mouth, then made me quickly drink the entire glass of mescal without stopping. I knew already that I had left the realm of observer and become a participant in the mystery unfolding around me.

The old man returned to the corner of the room, selected an old tequila bottle half full of cloudy amber liquid, left the room, then returned in a moment with the same bottle filled to the top. He placed the bottle on the floor in front of me, and began to intone prayers in Spanish that invoked his own personal power, my power and the power of the Christian and Nahua pantheons. I heard my ex-wife's name several times as Don Fidel blessed the bottle many times with circular and cross-like movements of his right hand. He finished, stood up, and told me to use the blessed liquid to sanctify my house, especially the doorways, whenever my ex-wife was present, or whenever she had caused some disharmony to enter our house.

I watched from another place as one of the shaman's assistants, a middle-aged Mayan-looking woman, began to brush every inch of Elvira's body with two bundles of thin branches of pepper tree with pink berries, some pine boughs, a tobacco leaf, and some yellow flowering rue, all the while chanting under her breath some kind of ritualistic prayer or incantation. Elvira raised her arms, spread her legs, and the woman swept every part of her body several times with the pungent-smelling bundles. After two or three minutes of brushing, the young woman waved the herb bundles in the air as if she were making a cross, then to the four compass points. When she was finished, she tossed the herbs and leaves in the corner of the room.

Then the woman repeated the process with an egg, sweeping Elvira's body accompanied by the same prayers, except this time she actually brushed the egg along Elvira's body as if she were palpating the surface of her skin, and when finished, she cracked the egg into a glass tumbler, held it up to the light to inspect it, then handed it to Don Fidel. He nodded, thought for a moment, then motioned for the woman to perform the same ritual cleansing of my body. When she was finished, Don Fidel handed me a characteristically-Mexican pink plastic bag filled with candles, plastic bottles of some kind of liquid, a very large tequila bottle full of scorpion liquid, small envelopes of powder, and two amulets to wear around our necks.

"Seven-hundred pesos please," the woman said politely in Spanish.

Seventy dollars seems a little pricey, I heard myself thinking to myself. I barely had time to walk back to the car and get helped into the back seat before I was suddenly transported internally to a world of spiritual focus, wordless, without the external distractions of any of my five senses as we drove home through some of the most beautiful scenery in all of Mexico. Amatlan is located outside of Tepoztlán, a place of power. Those who know say that the power comes from the earth's magnetic or gravitational energy that emerges from the ground in the mineral rich mountains there. Four hundred meters above the city there in the Tepoztéco hills the Aztecs built a pyramid dedicated to their god of the wind, Ehécatl. Sightings in the area and video corroboration of UFO's apparently riding on that same wind have increased in the last 5 years. New-age Mexicans recount how the remnants of ancient forgotten civilizations fled to Tepoztlán to await a coming millennium. Pancho Villa himself hid out during the Mexican Revolution and licked his wounds in the ancient hilltop ruins above Tepoztlán. The orange, red, and pink bougainvillea cover many of the buildings, and the color of the sky is unlike any intense blue of any sky anywhere. Yet the magic of the area did not distract me from the internal journey I took to find the resources I would use upon returning to California. In a few hours I returned to the external world as I finally understood and accepted my role as protector of my blessed wife, Elvira.

From that moment on, our struggle shifted from defensive to proactive. Letting go and saying, "No," became our tactic. *Un millón de Gracias,* Don Fidel. You saved our lives and our marriage.

Elvira returned again alone to Don Fidel two years later for a follow-up visit. She arrived home with candles, protective powders, herbs for baths and instructions about burying a photograph. Don Fidel had suggested that the only way to stop a rabid dog is to kill it. Elvira initially had warmed to the idea, but later she and I let go of the appealing but deadly thought after realizing that such a mortal intention would destroy more of our own love than all the hate any ex-wife could ever summon.

Point four.

We learned a profoundly useful lesson throughout this ordeal, namely, that letting go is usually better than grasping. The protracted and unsuccessful struggle to hold on to the two children (you know, joint physical custody) only created stress, disappointment, and suffering between Elvira and me. When we finally decided to let go of striving against the overwhelming tendency of the legal system to treat all ex-wife-mothers as victims, to treat all mothers as better parents than any father could be, then we returned to ourselves, blessed to have our sanity, energy, balance, and harmony back. The situation resolved itself with time, and we became students of life again. *Gracias a la vida que nos ha dado tanto.*

Lastly, point five.

Every dysfunctional family has the hero and the fuck-up. My first marriage was dysfunctional, and so both our lovely children quietly and imperceptibly assumed those two roles until divorce revealed the situation. My older son became identified tacitly as the fuck-up: he didn't do well in high school; he never could adjust to college work; he didn't stay at jobs a long time; he had no health insurance from employment; he bummed around the country several times; he let his hair and beard grow beyond the point of acceptability; he tended to form relationships with older women many of whom were needy and dysfunctional themselves; and he has slipped from time to time into grey shades of hypochondria. My older daughter is the heroic savior: she defended her mother during divorce; she graduated with honors from high school; she made her way without much support through university; she went to Panama in the Peace Corps and then extended another year training other volunteers; she completed her Masters in international micro-economics; she spent a summer in Guatemala training economists in-country; and she is now working for the Colorado DOT.

Yet time, being the sage master of all, thankfully has chamfered the edges of both fuck-up and hero. My son is making a living with his vibrant painting and his wonderful and unique music; he lives with a woman who loves and cares for him; he has no regular job; he visits Elvira, me, and his half-brother and sister regularly; he is full of love, enthusiasm, artistic talent, and the joy and melancholy of life. My daughter wisely dove into the world of helping others, and she came back from Latin America forgiving, swearing, easy-going, and more human. While less and less frequently they play out their antiquated roles from the disassembled dysfunction of our previous family/matrimonial incarnation, they are full, warm, loving children, human beings who love their mother, their father, their step-father, and Elvira.

> *Thank you for sharing your marriages and your children with me, including your help in the birthing. It doesn't surprise me that you would do that. In fact I'd be surprised if you didn't. It's obvious that you take well to being a husband and a father. Your wife and children are blest. Too many men make neither good husbands nor good fathers…You are thrice blest with Elvira and your children. That is <u>evangelion</u>, gospel, good news, something to be shared. Write about that. It is a rarity, and people need to know: marriage and family work. I am sure you are right: "Lack of parenting will be the downfall of civilization."* [lxii]

What more could anyone desire? Well, the fact that time has also eased and perhaps even removed the sharpness of my relationship with my ex-wife.

Enough said.

Thank you to all.

Chapter 13: Good-Bye, Narcissus

"They put him to bed and the physician stayed to examine him. He found him hopelessly ill." [lxiii]

"Sometimes he had a fever and was delirious; sometimes he was lucid, and then Narcissus was sent for each time. These last conversations with Goldmund became extremely important to him. Narcissus set down a few fragment of Goldmund's reports and confessions." [lxiv]

"What he murmured after that could not be understood. Those last two days Narcissus sat by his bed day and night, watching his life ebb away. Goldmund's last words burned like fire in his heart." [lxv]

Hermann Hesse
Narcissus and Goldmund

Many years ago the stream of your life and the stream of my life joined and ran together. Then we stopped sharing words. As the silence lengthened from one year to two to three to more, I couldn't help wondering if our waters hadn't parted, and if great stretches of land hadn't separated us again, as in the beginning. In one way we were never lost to each other. Our love had been running together all those years...I would think about you and feel about you and ache to hear you, to hold you, to read your writing, to know that you still loved me as I still loved you... I have carried you in my heart all these years, Chas. Don't expect anything very spiritual from me. I'm no Narcissus. Just a jaded old working man with nothing much to say. [lxvi]

Brother Paul Williams

SO ON FEBRUARY 28, 2001, thirty exiled years after that dark Good Friday when I decided to abandon the monastery and Narcissus for the call of the world, my dear wife, Elvira, our two children, Maya and Carlo, and I drove north one final time for Brother Paul's funeral at two o'clock in the afternoon a day after my 52nd birthday, February 27, 2001.

Hundreds of cars and pickups were parked everywhere along the one-lane road off of old Highway 99 leading into the New Clairvaux Abbey. As we walked into the monastery, we noticed the rows of cars parked on the grass, scores of people milling in groups here and there, and the monks visible in the guest house kitchen preparing food. Neither my wife nor our children had ever been to a monastery, so I began to point out some of the obvious features—the guest houses, the koi fishpond, the fields, the gravel roads, the church in the distance.

I searched for recognizable landmarks for my heart to grab. People were walking down the shaded road towards the church, monks also were beginning to bicycle slowly towards the church, and suddenly someone grabbed my arm from the rear.

"I am so happy to see that you could make it to the funeral, Charles..." Brother John Cullen embraced me quickly, and raised his eyebrows to be introduced to my family.

"Why don't you all follow me."

Funerals in the Trappist-Cistercian tradition are stark affairs—a wooden coffin made of simple wooden boards, the unembalmed body uncovered in the coffin, a procession into the church, Mass, and then a slow procession to the graveyard. Normally lay people (non-monks) are not allowed into the monastic cloister, but Brother Paul had gathered so many friends locally and from all over the country that the abbot had permitted everyone— and that meant in this case about five-hundred people—to come into the church and the cloister and the cemetery for their dear Brother Paul's funeral.

Everyone walked solemnly from the church to the monastery cemetery located a few hundred yards from the monastery buildings, in a peaceful large grass covered area surrounded and enclosed all around by tall cypress trees. When you enter the confines of the cemetery, you immediately feel the peace of the monastic setting and lifestyle. The six monks carrying the bier with Brother Paul arrived along with the abbot and the six priest-monks and the twenty or so brother-monks. Everyone else began filling in around the area leaving about a twenty foot radius circle around what everyone there was staring at—the open grave already dug and waiting. No one spoke, no one whispered, no baby cried, and everyone waited while the monks made ready to bury their friend and brother.

Suddenly Brother John Cullen pulled a simple wooden ladder from out of hiding, placed the ladder down into the open grave, and proceeded to actually climb down into the dark hole. Each man, woman, and child withheld their shock and disbelief until a few minutes later the somber monk climbed back out without any apparent explanation to those of us who did not know why he did such an odd thing.

The prayers began, the abbot relating events about Brother Paul's long life in the monastery, intoning the death prayers, droning a psalm or two for the dead, waiting for everyone there to answer, "Amen." I noticed that Brother Paul's brother, who had played The Green Hornet in the 1960's TV program, was standing close to the grave, in sun glasses, unknown to those around him. Then Brother John nodded his head, began climbing down into the grave again, and motioned to the pallbearers who lifted Paul's body from the bier and brought him over to where Brother John was half-hidden and clearly ready to place the body directly into the ground without a coffin.

I saw Brother John take my dear friend, Brother Paul's, body clothed in his simple black and white habit into his arms and carry him alone down into the deep hole in the earth. He disappeared into the grave, and it was simple courtesy and fear that prevented people watching from gasping out loud. As the abbot began a final prayer, the wind suddenly and unexpectedly started to blow, the tops of the thin cypress trees began to sway, and as the wind rushed over the graveyard, leaves and pine needles from all the trees in the area began whirling mysteriously around the small protected cemetery area, and an eerily loud whooshing sound swirled and engulfed the entire group of mourners there for a minute as unseen, Brother John adjusted his friend's final resting place in the ground—covering his face, touching his face or heart perhaps, saying his personal prayer, then emerging from the dark underworld as the wind itself, and millions of leaves settled on the ground and on our heads.

Everyone was silent because the Spirit of the living and the dead had visited us all to carry Paul's spirit and body away and to remind us of our own imminent departure. After a few minutes of unearthly hush, Brother John reached down and picked up a shovel. He thrust it into the pile of fresh earth, and threw a shovelful into the grave. Monk after monk did the same, and then each guest took their own turn to return the dust to dust. Then I, then Elvira, then Maya, then Carlo. A final prayer, and it was finished. No one moved for a timeless moment, then without another word, each person shifted in place and began to walk away from the strange miracle they had just experienced. Monks returned each their own way to the shelter of the cloister, astonished and muted guests arrived quietly one by one at the guest house and their cars, and we followed without saying a word about what we had just witnessed.

We drank a sociable glass or two of juice or coffee, ate a cookie or two in the guest house area, but there was no one there to say good-bye to, no one we knew, nothing else to do, so we followed the river of cars back out to Highway 99 to our room in the Days Inn at Corning five miles away. I was grateful that my dear family had visited the scene of my youth, my coming of spiritual age, my time with Brother Paul, my Narcissus. I would return countless times to the monastery in my heart and in my dreams, but I would never again return to this monastery.

While driving back to Salinas from the monastery, I recalled the time a few weeks earlier when I had walked into the infirmary room where a still breathing Brother Paul lay unconscious waiting for me to make our good-byes. I had paused there a moment, wondering what would be appropriate in such unusual circumstances, thinking about what I would say to my friend, assuming some part of him could hear me, imagining that his breathing would change when he sensed my presence.

"I love you, Paul. Thank you for being my dear, dear friend. Thank you for being my Narcissus and for letting me be your Goldmund forever. I love you, Paul. I will remember you forever. Thank you, thank you, thank you…"

I had had put my hand on his heart, felt the rhythmic movement of his body as he was slipping away so slowly from this earth and from all those who loved him. I felt my hand on his heart as I repeated the mantra of love. When it was finally time to leave a few minutes and a lifetime later, I turned, strode resolutely out the infirmary door, walked down to my room in the guest house, packed my few things quickly, said nothing to no one, and began the long drive home alone.

> Abbey of New Clairvaux
> 28 Feb 01
>
> Dear Charles,
> Thank you for coming for the Mass & Burial & for bringing your family. And thank you for the generous check in memory of Paul B for the library. We appreciate this. I know he does too from his place "with God". I was not aware that you were present & I regret this as I would have liked to meet you & the family. May the Blessings of Peace be with you — Thomas Davis, Abbot

Chapter 14: Epilogue

I'm glad that you plugged us into that archetype long ago, and I'm anxious to plunge back into it once again. I wonder what the new reading of <u>Narcissus and Goldmund</u> will mean for each of us and for the "we" that started those many years ago. No doubt our reading will lead us back to those earlier days when we were younger and full of youthful passion, and you were here, and life was ahead of us with vistas unlimited. Little did we realize then how symbolic <u>Narcissus and Goldmund</u> would actually become for us. [lxvii]

Brother Paul Williams

SO, FITTINGLY, THIS IS THE END OF THE STORY of my odyssey with my Narcissus. Not the chronological end, of course, but the physical culmination certainly. I assume that you have put together the puzzle pieces of flash-backs, foreshadowing, repetitions, and shifts in time and place authors love to utilize so their story isn't just a predictable one-way, one-lane road to an obvious destination on a tenuous map in a reader's mind. Memoirs are mini-lifetimes, metaphors for one's life. Memoirists are fortunate to be able to relive their lives through their writing, and more wonderfully, we are forced to make some kind of sense of the events we've chosen to include in our memoirs. Patterns emerge in the writing of a memoir—patterns of choice, events, actions and consequences, friendships, love relationships, mistakes and missteps. When we humans look back on our lives and see patterns—both constructive and destructive, we can change, adjust, or maintain the course of our lives in order to get the best result, have the good life we envision, be happy and content with ourselves and our lives.

The two men I loved so deeply have enabled me to explore the patterns of masculinity I think are truly powerful. I believe men need other, deeper, more constructive ways of being with each other. The strengths of men are not marshalled and deployed best through sports or politics. Brother Paul was the first person I loved with passion, my deepest spiritual friend and guide, a creative and strong man who found his struggle to be human in the silence he cultivated as a monk. He showed me how human beings embody both flesh and spirit, and that flesh and spirit are both of God and so good. Doctor David and I had the highest of times alone together in the mountains, making wild and beautiful creations in my workshop, cooking outrageous food in our kitchens, casting concrete, and planting bamboo in our garden. That man taught me so easily how to be open to every person, to act as if I knew each person, and to connect with each person's human heart in a simple and direct way. In those two men my sense of what a man is has been synthesized into the kind of man I try to be each day. The fact that those two men are gone moves me even more to become daily the kind of man that reverberates to their frequencies.

The few women I have loved deeply have taught me unintentionally about the selfless giving of affection and the generous receiving of a man's need for grounding in a woman. I learned about both animal and spiritual passion, the confusion of emotional disharmony, the pain of unfulfilled expectations, the resentment of being left for another and the power of leaving the other for freedom, and the uniqueness of each woman's body self-expressed in movement, gesture, attitude, and touch. The beauty and exquisite delicacy of each woman's contours, surface, angles, valleys, and secret hiding places challenge even the best writer to describe the marvelous gift that is each woman.

The vivacious young girl who strode into my classroom over twenty-five years ago back at the beginning of chapter ten became the most beautiful woman I have ever known, my wife, my teacher, my best friend, my lover, my true counselor, and my life companion. It's not fashionable to say the word "soul-mate," but in our case it is most true. Of course, I think we were not "destined from the beginning of time." I do think for some deep atomic-level reason we came together with much giving and much receiving in our hearts and souls, giving and receiving with each other. I have felt the most passion, suffered the deepest, injured the most callously, needed the most intensely, learned the most about being human, and given the most of myself ever to my wife, Elvira.

She—the axis around which I revolve, the wick I burn, the flower I tend, the mirror into which I peer, the mystery I probe, the earth into which I dig—so many metaphors to describe what we have become with each other. We survived work, money, moving, construction, friends, emotional crises, parents, siblings, deaths, and childrearing. We look forward to what we will make of our later years together, following our noses forward with trust, eagerness, and joy.

Hand in hand I have tried always to live on the deepest level possible in everything I have done. I discovered immeasurable joy in the passion and challenge of loving a small number of people in my life, and in the last third of my life, one in particular. I am sure that at the very end, when my consciousness withdraws from my bodily senses and then from my mind, and comes to rest in my heart, the things I have done in my life will not matter—sports, hobbies, travel, job, writing, music, food, adventure, this memoir, none will matter. When I leave my body behind to be reabsorbed into The Self, I will be conscious for the last time first of the few people I have loved and who have loved me, of my Narcissus, Brother Paul, and then finally, of my beloved wife. No fear of extinction, just the certainty of returning again somehow to unknowable undifferentiated Bliss where they will be.

Chapter 15: A Small Miracle

> "'So you did think of me?' Narcissus asked softly. Goldmund answered just as softly: 'Oh yes, Narcissus, I have thought of you. Always, always'" [lxviii]
> Hermann Hesse
> *Narcissus and Goldmund*

DURING THE INITIAL STAGE OF THIS BOOK I spent several days word processing the many quotations from *Narcissus and Goldmund* that I had highlighted and underlined over decades of reading and rereading, planning on using some of them as epigraphs at the beginning of chapters or as textual punctuation marks throughout my own narrative journey to show the wonderful similarity between Narcissus and Goldmund's friendship and journey and my own odyssey with Brother Paul. In the hours of contemplative word processing, very much like medieval monks methodically copying biblical manuscripts, I came to relive in my heart all the internal and external events from my friendship with Brother Paul.

When I came to the last few pages where Goldmund has returned to Mariabronn monastery a broken and dying man, and Narcissus is tending to him, listening to his dying words—

> "But how will you die when your time comes, Narcissus, since you have no mother? Without a mother, one cannot love. Without a mother, one cannot die." [lxix]

> "What he murmured after that could not be understood. Those last two days Narcissus sat by his bed day and night, watching his life ebb away. Goldmund's last words burned like fire in his heart." [lxx]

—I felt suddenly in the depths of my heart Brother Paul's life and death and my own experience at his dying side. I broke down in tears and sobbed deeply, feeling his own heart and spirit expressed in his life and in our friendship.

I've broken down emotionally, cried, and sobbed my heart out before. This time I experienced something I have never known before. Suddenly, as I cried and sobbed, my little home office where I was working started to spin and rotate, as everything I saw, everything actually there, including my own entire self, whirled three-dimensionally like an expanding galaxy, first slowly, then increasingly faster and faster. I felt that I was being pulled into an actual other physical dimension. After thirty seconds I struggled to sit up, tried unsuccessfully to stop sobbing, as I felt myself being essentially dissolved into something much vaster than myself and the office, something solid and physical that was on the verge of The Cosmos dispersing my body back into Itself.

I stood up awkwardly, rubbed my head and arms to try to shake off what I thought was nausea, but I continued to feel myself being dissolved, taken away, by some unknown, commanding, all-encompassing force. I stumbled into the bedroom and lay down, trying to come back to my familiar three-dimensional reality. After ten minutes, I sat up, walked around, and saw the inside of my house as it was still there, real, not spinning any more. All day I felt as if I had barely avoided being pulled back into the unmanifested realm of being. For several hours I tried to bring back into wholeness the emotional and physical parts of myself that had been pulled at and almost dissolved. I sensed almost immediately that the explanation for such a mysterious and remarkable experience was that Brother Paul had come back one final time to visit his dear friend, his Goldmund, Brother Charles.

I realized to my surprise that I had never mourned for Paul, never cried out in grief for his death. Brother Paul had certainly visited me one last time so that we could mourn together for the loss of each other in life. I recounted to my wife that evening what had happened, and while I spoke, my emotions flooded my heart again. She agreed that he must have come to visit, said his final good-bye, and given his approval—his blessing, I think—for this book about our friendship that I had just started to write by immersing myself in the intimate recapitulation of our odyssey through the faithful copying of the poignant events from Narcissus and Goldmund's story. So strange and wonderful that a similar whirling spirit-wind stirred and engulfed everyone at Brother Paul's interment at the monastery. The word for wind in Greek, *pneuma*, means breath, spirit, wind. I will always remember that powerful experience as an affirmation that the potent harmonization that love can create between people and so in the cosmos exists in Reality everywhere and forever, limitless and without dimension.

So now, at the end of this memoir, as you reflect back on a true tale of friendship, love, and cosmic harmonization, remember that *you* yourself are part of this magnificent process that is both in and out of time and place.

The power of attraction and harmonization.

So let go, and follow the flickering light that you feel within.

This light *is* you.

Chapter 16: The Last Word

"Now I see that it was really so, that you really do love me. But I have always loved you, Narcissus. Half of my life was spent courting you. I knew that you, too, were fond of me, but I never dared hope that you would tell me some day, you're such a proud man. You give me your love in this moment when I have nothing left, when wandering and freedom, world and women have abandoned me. I accept it and I thank you for it." [lxxi]

Hermann Hesse
Narcissus and Goldmund

You see that I neither scoff or fail to listen. How could I scoff or fail to listen? Whatever you say always means much to me because YOU mean much to me. Over the years, we've not said many words to each other, but the little we've said has had a richness that makes me cherish your words and the man, the friend, the lover and the brother who has strung the words together. Ironically, most of our words have been words about the inadequacy of words! So how in the world can you write about a friendship like that? [lxxii]

Brother Paul Williams
My Narcissus

Endnotes

i   Hesse, Herman. *Narcissus and Goldmund*. Trans. Ursule Molinaro. New York. Bantam Books Published With Arrangement With Farrar, Straus And Giroux, Inc. 1968. 270.

ii   Personal correspondence between Brother Paul Williams and Charles Frode

iii   My own copy is highlighted, underlined, and stuffed with sticky markers. It has assumed the status of a scripture of sorts as it has travelled with me for the past forty years. All quotations are taken from that edition:

- Hesse, Herman. *Narcissus and Goldmund*. Trans. Ursule Molinaro. New York. Bantam Books Published With Arrangement With Farrar, Straus And Giroux, Inc. 1968

iv   Hesse, 311.
v   Hesse, 311.
vi   Hesse, 311.
vii   Hesse, 306.
viii   Personal correspondence
ix   Hesse, 43.
x   Personal correspondence
xi   Hesse, 272.
xii   Hesse, 273.
xiii   Personal correspondence
xiv   *Ishi in Two Worlds* (1961) by the anthropologist Theodora Kroeber, the wife of Alfred Kroeber
xv   Hesse, 1.
xvi   Hesse, 1.
xvii   Personal correspondence
xviii   Hesse, 2.
xix   Personal correspondence
xx   Psalm 41, *The Psalms*, A New Translation, Fontana Books, 1963
xxi   Hesse, 15.
xxii   Personal correspondence
xxiii   Hesse, 155.
xxiv   Personal correspondence
xxv   Hesse, 39.
xxvi   Hesse, 56.
xxvii   Personal correspondence
xxviii   Hesse, 63.
xxix   Personal correspondence
xxx   Pictures taken from http://nqking.wordpress.com/ and http://www.home-temple.org/Bishop_Lewis2.jpg respectively
xxxi   *The Bhagavad Gita*. Eknath Easwaran, translator. Tomales, California. Nilgiri Press. 1985. 2:55. p.67

[xxxii] Hesse, 65.
[xxxiii] Hesse, 66.
[xxxiv] Personal correspondence
[xxxv] Hesse, 42.
[xxxvi] Personal correspondence
[xxxvii] Hesse, 246.
[xxxviii] Hesse, 307.
[xxxix] Hesse, 77.
[xl] Hesse, 80.
[xli] Hesse, 99.
[xlii] Hesse, 100.
[xliii] Hesse, 167.
[xliv] Hesse, 167.
[xlv] Hesse, 168.
[xlvi] Hesse, 246-247.
[xlvii] Personal correspondence
[xlviii] Personal correspondence
[xlix] Personal correspondence
[l] Merton, Thomas. *Hagia Sophia*
[li] Hesse, 193.
[lii] Hesse, 160.
[liii] Hesse, 169.
[liv] Hesse, 76.
[lv] Personal correspondence
[lvi] Hesse, 96.
[lvii] Hesse, 95.
[lviii] Hesse, 96.
[lix] Personal correspondence
[lx] Hesse, 290.
[lxi] Personal correspondence
[lxii] Personal correspondence
[lxiii] Hesse, 305.
[lxiv] Hesse, 305.
[lxv] Hesse, 312.
[lxvi] Personal correspondence
[lxvii] Personal correspondence
[lxviii] Hesse, 262.
[lxix] Hesse, 311.
[lxx] Hesse, 312.
[lxxi] Hesse, 307.
[lxxii] Personal correspondence

Printed in Great Britain
by Amazon